MEXICAN
MAIN DISHES

★ ★ ★ ★ ★

MEXICAN MAIN DISHES

TORTILLAS, TAMALES, FAJITAS, ENCHILADAS AND MORE!

MARLENA SPIELER

APPLE

A QUINTET BOOK

Published by The Apple Press
6 Blundell Street
London N7 9BH

ISBN 1-85076-652-5

This book was designed and produced by
Quintet Publishing Limited
6 Blundell Street
London N7 9BH

Creative Director: Richard Dewing
Designer: Ian Hunt
Project Editor: Stefanie Foster
Text Editor: Diana Vowles
Illustrator: Joanne Makin

Typeset in Great Britain by
Central Southern Typesetters, Eastbourne
Manufactured by
J. Film Process, Singapore, Pte Ltd
Printed by Star Standard Industries (Pte) Ltd, Singapore

ACKNOWLEDGEMENTS

A warm thank you to those who sampled my recipes, enjoying the successes and good-naturedly putting up with the dishes that didn't quite make it. To my daughter Leah for her continual enthusiasm for the pleasures of the table, especially the Mexican table. To my step-daughter Gretchen, with whom I have shared many late-night carnitas quesadillas picnics; to my husband Alan McLaughlan for his stamina and creative shopping; to Peter Milne for his appreciation and delicious food ideas; to Jon Harford for his vegetarian sensibility in recipe testing; to Hoops and everyone at Outdoor Chef, where the grilled and barbecued dishes were tested on the marvellous gas barbecue.

Jerome Freeman and Sheila Hannon, Amanda Hamilton and Tim Hemmeter, Christine and Maureen Smith, Nigel and Graham, Esther Novack and John Chendo, Fiona Beckett, Kathleen Griffen, Sheila Dillon, Kamala Friedman, Sandy Waks, Trish Robinson, Michelle Schmidt, Simon Parkes, Michael Bauer, M.A. and Richard Mariner for the tortilla press,

Paula Levine for the tortillas, Jill Vaux, Vanessa Welch, Etty and Bruce Blackman, Paul Richardson, Susan Redgrave, Helene and Robin Simpson, the Wight family, Lena Gilbert and Jason Gaber all tucked in to various dishes and helped in the testing, even if they weren't aware of it at the time. Thanks to Jackie Higuera McMahan, for her company one lovely afternoon in San Francisco's Mission District. Thanks, too, to my lovely cat Freud, though having a cat who insists his food bowl is garnished with fresh coriander and accompanied by tortillas is as annoying as it is amusing.

Thanks to my parents, Caroline and Izzy Smith, Aunt Estelle and Uncle Sy Opper, and Grandmother Sophia Dubowsky who whetted my appetite for Mexican food when I was young and vulnerable to this delicious life-long addiction.

And to Stefanie Foster and Quintet Publishing for commissioning me to write this book.

CONTENTS

INTRODUCTION
6

GLOSSARY AND BASIC TECHNIQUES
7

CHAPTER ONE
TORTILLAS, BEANS AND SALSAS
9

CHAPTER TWO
SIMMERED MEATS, BROTHS AND TAMALES
20

CHAPTER THREE
**CASSEROLES, EGG DISHES
AND VEGETARIAN MEALS**
32

CHAPTER FOUR
BARBECUED AND GRILLED FOODS
47

CHAPTER FIVE
**BRAISED, STEWED
AND ROASTED DISHES**
58

INDEX
80

INTRODUCTION

Sitting down to the *comida corrida*, or main meal, in Mexico is one of the great moments of each day, for what could be more enticing than great platters of this hearty, usually spicy, food?

While the meal begins with soup, or antojitos or botonas, it is the main courses that form the real meal. You might find a simmering cazuela of chicken and vegetables, perfumed with spices and coloured with bright red chilli purée, or a potful of meats and vegetables, such as turkey mole, to be eaten as both the soup and main course.

Often dinner will be cooked on the grill to give smoky, succulent, and irresistible flavours and textures. You might find strips of beef (fajitas), golden marinated chicken, brick-hued fish, all spicy morsels meant to be rolled up in an exquisitely fresh tortilla.

A main course Mexicana might also consist of a deep tureen of robust soup such as posole, rich with starchy hominy and meaty chunks of pork, its salady garnish providing a fresh contrast, or a casserole filled with enchiladas, or chilaquiles (tortillas layered and baked with chilli sauces into a savoury delectable mush.) Paella, roasted meats or poultry, braised fish – all may be the main plate.

This book is full of such main courses, or *platillos fuertes*, from that vast and fascinating land. From the lush tropical reaches of the Yucatan to the northern arid plains of Sonora and the beaches and vineyards of Baja, each region is represented by its own distinctive flavours and perfumes.

NOTE: While none of the recipes are difficult there are several somewhat unusual cooking techniques that form a particular culinary language. Once you are familiar with the processes you will find them easy.

> • Puréeing sauces then "frying" in a small amount of oil until the mixture intensifies, before adding stock and other ingredients.
>
> • Toasting and roasting vegetables such as onions, tomatoes, garlic and chillies, before puréeing into sauces.
>
> • Toasting and grinding dried chillies into powders.
>
> • Toasting, soaking and puréeing dried chillies into sauces.

GLOSSARY

CHILLIES

Capsicum frutescens, otherwise known as chillies, or hot peppers, come in so wide a variety they are nearly impossible to categorize. However, there are some basic guidelines to help us with the chillies that are more easily available outside of Mexico.

WHENEVER USING CHILLIES, TAKE CARE. WASH YOUR HANDS IMMEDIATELY AFTER USING, AND DO NOT TOUCH YOUR EYES OR OTHER SENSITIVE AREAS AS THE VOLATILE OILS LINGER AND LINGER. TO PREVENT YOUR HANDS FROM BURNING FOR DAYS AFTER HANDLING CHILLIES, USE RUBBER GLOVES.

WHEN HEATING CHILLIES IN A PAN, OR WHIRLING THEM IN A BLENDER OR FOOD PROCESSOR, DO NOT INHALE OR PLACE YOUR FACE NEAR THE LID WHEN REMOVING IT. INHALING CHILLI FUMES CAN BE VERY PAINFUL AND DISTRESSING. CHILDREN ARE PARTICULARLY SUSCEPTIBLE AND SHOULD NOT BE IN THE SAME ROOM WITH FRYING CHILLIES.

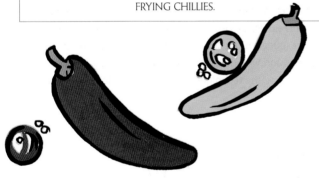

Chillies come fresh or dried. Fresh they are bright and full flavoured, most often available in green, but red and sometimes yellow varieties are also found. Generally, with a few explosive exceptions, the smaller the chilli the hotter.

Tiny Thai, or bird's eye chillies are very very hot, serranos on the hotter side of medium, while the larger Kenya, or jalapeño, are hot but not impossible. The jalapeño type chillies are probably the most useful all-purpose chilli, for their pleasant flavour and bearable heat. The poblano chilli looks much like an ordinary green pepper and is on the milder side as chillies go; it is lovely for stuffing. The most widely available exception to the "small is hottest" rule is the Scots bonnet, a lantern shaped chilli in parrot-like hues of red, yellow, green and orange that is breathtakingly, aggressively hot. This is one of the most readily available of chillies, and care should be taken to acclimatize yourself to its tropical heat.

Fresh green chillies may be used raw, cooked, or roasted, then added to sauces, stews, etc.

Dried chillies come in a wide range of types such as pasilla, ancho, guajillo, puya, cascabel, and so on. These are the chillies used to make "mild chilli powder". To make your own mild chilli powder lightly toast whichever chilli you desire, then cut off the stems and remove the seeds. Cut the lightly toasted chilli into small pieces and whirl in a coffee grinder until it forms a powder. Storebought mild chilli powder may be mixed with paprika and used in place of the individual chillies in sauces.

CHIPOTLE CHILLI

This is the dried, smoked jalapeño, fiery hot and scented with smoke. It is available dried or in tins, "en adobo", a spicy marinade. A recipe for chipotles en adobo is in the Salsa chapter.

JALAPEÑOS EN ESCABECHE

These pickled chillies are delicious with refried beans and cheese, or tucked into any taco or torta. Widely available.

TOMATILLOS

Green husk tomatoes with a sour flavour and a crisp texture. They must be husked and blanched before using, as raw they are not so delightful as when tender and ready to be puréed into sauces. Since they add a tart accent, occasionally unsweetened gooseberries or a handful of shredded sorrel, or a big squeeze of lemon and a few underripe tomatoes can take their place.

NOPALES

Cactus pads, an unusual green vegetable doted on throughout Mexico. Must be peeled and blanched first to rid them of their sticky juices (much like okra). Occasionally available fresh in West Indian markets; imported from Mexico in tins. If unavailable, use blanched green beans tossed with a few drops of vinegar, onion and oregano.

SOME MEXICAN COOKING METHODS

ROASTING AND PEELING CHILLIES

Place chillies of any sort over a flame and cook, lightly charring the skin, turning until evenly charred. If using small chillies, place them in an ungreased frying pan instead or skewer them before placing on flame. When evenly and lightly charred place in a plastic bag or in the bottom of a saucepan. Seal the bag or place the lid on the pan and leave for 30–60 minutes. Remove and use a paring knife to peel off the skin. Cut off and discard the stem and remove the seeds.

TOASTING GARLIC AND ONIONS

Place unpeeled garlic cloves in a heavy ungreased frying pan and cook over medium heat until cloves char lightly and turn soft inside; turn several times so that they cook evenly. Remove from pan. To use, squeeze from skin. Use the cooked flesh and discard the skin. Onions may be toasted by cutting them unpeeled (or peeled, as desired) in half, then placing the cut pieces on an ungreased pan and cooking over medium heat until charred. Remove and use the flesh as desired.

REHYDRATING CHILLIES

Lightly toast dried chillies by holding them over a flame or tossing them in a heavy ungreased pan over medium low heat. Place in a bowl and cover with boiling water. Let sit 30–45 minutes until chillies are soft, then either purée and sieve, or scrape away the flesh from the papery skin (which should then be discarded).

MASHING GARLIC

To extract full flavour from garlic, use a mortar and pestle; add a pinch of salt before crushing.

ROASTING TOMATOES

Place tomatoes in a baking dish and drizzle with oil and salt. Bake in a medium hot oven for 45 minutes or until they shrink and concentrate in flavour. Let cool in their juices then remove skins and squeeze to extract the flavourful juices in the skins. Discard squeezed out skins and combine with the flesh of the tomatoes and with the pan juices. Tomatoes may also be toasted, using the technique described for onions and garlic.

CHAPTER ONE

TORTILLAS, BEANS AND SALSAS

★ ★ ★ ★ ★

TORTILLAS, BEANS AND SALSAS

Along with rice, tortillas and beans form the basics of the Mexican kitchen. Most everyday meals are based on those foods, along with a bowl of salsa to spice it up, whatever vegetables the garden or market may yield, and perhaps some braised, simmered or grilled meat, poultry or fish.

CORN TORTILLAS

Fresh tortillas are the basis of Mexican cuisine: the flat cakes of pounded lime-slaked corn have a distinctive flavour and texture like no other food I know. Tortillas are not only the bread of Mexico, they are the plates and knives and forks as well. Tortillas wrap up tacos and enchiladas, and are served with barbecues, for impromptu tacos. They are served as a snack, or as a bread accompaniment alongside the *comida corrida*, or midday dinner.

MAKES 12 14CM/6IN TORTILLAS OR 24 7CM/3IN TORTILLAS

450g/1lb masa harina	175–250ml/6–8fl oz water at warm room temperature (less if weather is humid)

1. Mix the flour with the water until it forms a soft but not gummy dough.
2. Take several plastic bags and cut the sides so that each forms a large rectangle. Heat a heavy frying pan or comal; I find that using two at a time makes the task quicker.
3. Roll a piece of dough into a ball about 3.5cm/1⅛in in diameter; place this ball on one side of a plastic rectangle, then place this rectangle on to the open tortilla press. Cover the other side with a plastic rectangle.
4. Close the press and push the handle down evenly and hard. Open it up and take the tortilla out of the press, picking up the whole thing carefully, then peel off the plastic and plop the tortilla directly into the hot pan. Lightly oiled hands makes the dough easier to handle.

5. Cook each tortilla quickly, about 2 minutes in total. When cooking the first side, wait for the edges to appear dry, then turn over and cook the second side until it is lightly speckled. Turn over and cook the first side a few more moments, then stack on a plate, and keep warm, covered with a clean cloth. Tortillas may puff up as they cook; this is a good sign, indicating a light, well-cooked tortilla.

REHEATING PURCHASED TORTILLAS

1. Lightly spray each tortilla with water and let them rest for a few minutes while you heat a lightly oiled heavy-based frying pan.
2. Put the whole stack of tortillas in it. When the bottom tortilla is warm, turn the whole stack using a spatula, so that the bottom tortilla is now the top one.
3. Cover and allow to cook in the steam for a few moments, then repeat, dividing the stack of tortillas from the middle. Each tortilla should be exposed to both the heat of the bottom of the pan and the steam that rises to the top.
4. Remove from the pan, place on a plate and cover with a clean cloth, sides folded over to keep the tortillas soft and warm.

NUTRITIONAL INFORMATION			
	TOTAL FAT	SAT FAT	CHOL	ENERGY
Total	16.5g	0mg	0mg	1840kcals/7700kJ
Per 6"	1.4g	0mg	0mg	153kcals/642kJ
Per 3–4"	0.7g	0mg	0mg	77kcals/321kJ

TOSTADAS

Stale tortillas make the crispest tostadas as they absorb less oil in the frying. Tostadas are oil-"toasted" tortillas, crisp as a cracker and very versatile. Whole, a tostada can form the basis for a one-portion dish. Spread with refried beans or sprinkle with cheese and melt the top, and serve with fresh crunchy salad, salsa, and herbs.

LOWER FAT TOSTADAS

Brush stale tortillas with vegetable oil and place on a baking sheet in a preheated oven at 220°C/425°F/Gas Mark 7. Bake until crisp and golden and lightly browned in places, about 15 minutes. Alternatively, bake in the oven at 150°C/300°F/Gas Mark 3 for 45 minutes or so. The long slow bake gives a crisper, more brittle crunch to the tostadas. Remove and place on a dry surface.

TRADITIONAL TOSTADAS

Fry the tortillas, one at a time, in shallow vegetable oil or melted lard, until crisp and golden-brown. Remove from the pan and drain on paper towels, then place on a dry surface. Keep warm in the oven at 180°C/350°F/Gas Mark 4 for up to 10 minutes: lower the heat to 140°C/275°F/Gas Mark 1 if keeping warm for up to 1 hour.

TOTOPOS (TORTILLA CHIPS)

Cut tortillas into wedges and prepare as for Tostadas . Use for chilaquiles, nachos, or for tortilla soup.

FAT-FREE TOTOPOS

Wet the tortillas one at a time and cut into wedges. Sprinkle with salt if desired. Arrange in a single layer on a non-stick baking sheet then baking in a preheated oven at 250°C/500°F/Gas Mark 10 for 4 minutes. Turn with a spatula or tongs and continue baking until golden-brown and crisp, about 3 minutes.
These will keep in an airtight container for two weeks.

TORTILLAS DE HARINA
FLOUR TORTILLAS

Flour tortillas are slightly chewy, lightly flecked from the pan, and delicious with chillied stews, barbecued meats, or wrapped around frijoles refritos and cheese for a hefty burrito.

MAKES 10-12 20CM/8IN TORTILLAS

100g/4oz lard or 120ml/4fl oz vegetable oil

450g/1lb plain flour (preferably white unbleached), sifted

250ml/8fl oz lukewarm water

2 tsp salt

1. Work the lard or oil into the flour with your fingers or in a food processor until it forms a crumb-like mixture.

2. Mix the water and salt, then stir into the flour.

3. Knead the dough for about 3 minutes or until it is no longer sticky. Cover and set aside for at least 2 hours or overnight.

4. Knead the dough again, then roll into small balls. For 18cm/7in tortillas make 5cm/2in balls, 36cm/14in tortillas will need balls about 7.5cm/3in in diameter.

5. Place each ball on a floured board, then roll into a 18cm/7in round, turning the dough so that the round becomes paper-thin.

6. Heat an ungreased heavy-based frying pan, griddle or comal until it is very hot. Place a flat dough round on the hot surface. Leave it for 20–30 seconds – if it puffs up, flatten it again with the back of a spatula.

7. Turn and cook on the other side for about 10 seconds. Transfer to a plate and keep covered with a clean cloth while you prepare the rest of the dough. The tortillas should be soft and flexible.

8. To use, reheat on the griddle before filling, etc.

NUTRITIONAL INFORMATION				
	TOTAL FAT	SAT FAT	CHOL	ENERGY
Total	130g	51g	116mg	2819kcals/111829kJ
10–12 8in	13g–11g	5g–4g	12g–10g	282kcals/1183kJ
				235kcals/986kJ

FRIJOLES

BEANS

Throughout Mexico, a pot sits on each backburner, bubbling away quietly, yielding up its contents of tender beans that accompany nearly every main course and also form fillings for many of the tortilla-based antojitos.
The liquid used for cooking beans is added to soups and stews, and is used to cook rice. (Arroz negro, rice cooked in black bean liquor, is startlingly grey in colour but very savoury and satisfying to eat.)
The colour, size and shape of the beans depends on where in Mexico you are. In general, black beans are eaten in the southern, more tropical regions, pink and pinto beans further north. Little white beans are served in the Yucatan, and big lima-like beans in Tarasca.

FRIJOLES REFRITOS

REFRIED BEANS

Despite the name "refried", frijoles refritos is not fried twice – rather it is puréed and heated in a small amount of hot fat, more or less fried once. I have heard it said that it is with typical south-of-the-border exuberance that many things are exaggerated, even the number of times the beans are fried!

SERVES 6 – 8

1 quantity Frijoles de Olla (page 12) made with pinto, pinquito, or other pink beans

1–2 onions, chopped

45ml/3tbsp vegetable oil

½tsp ground cumin

½tsp mild chilli powder

salt

1. Mash or purée the beans to a coarse, chunky consistency. Leave some whole, others in pieces, still others puréed into a thick sauce-like mixture.
2. Fry the onion in the vegetable oil until softened and lightly browned, then sprinkle in the cumin and chilli powder.
3. Ladle in a scoop of the bean mixture, cook over medium-high heat until thickened and slightly darkened in colour, then add another ladleful of the beans and repeat until all the beans have simmered into a thick, darkened, flavourful mixture.
4. Season with salt to taste.

NUTRITIONAL INFORMATION				
	TOTAL FAT	SAT FAT	CHOL	ENERGY
Total	60g	13g	45mg	2309kcals/9755kJ
Serves 6	10g	2g	8mg	385kcals/1626kJ
Serves 8	7.5g	1.5mg	6mg	289kcals/1219kJ

VARIATION

FRIJOLES REFRITOS CON QUESO

Top refried pinto or other pink beans with about 175g/6oz coarsely grated mild white cheese and either heat in the oven or stir in. Let the cheese melt then serve.

FRIJOLES DE OLLA

SIMMERED BEANS

The green herb epazote, said to help mitigate the embarrassing effects of beans, is usually added to the pot of simmering beans. A leaf or two of mint, while not the same thing, gives a similar flavour and wind-easing result.
Use these beans as an accompaniment, to make frijoles refritos, or anywhere simmered beans are called for. A bowl of warm frijoles de olla, along with a few warm tortillas and a chilli or two, is the mainstay of the Mexican diet.

FRIJOLES BORRACHOS
DRUNKEN BEANS

S E R V E S   6 – 8

1 onion, chopped	½–1 fresh green chilli such as jalapeño, thinly sliced
3 cloves garlic, chopped	250ml/8fl oz flavourful beer, or as desired
100g/4oz bacon, diced	
5 tomatoes, diced	1 quantity Frijoles de Olla (page 12)
½ green pepper or mild green chilli, coarsely chopped	salt and pepper

1. Place the onion, garlic and bacon in a frying pan and slowly fry until the bacon is crisp and onions soft.

2. Add the tomatoes, pepper and chilli and continue to cook until thickened and sauce-like.

3. Purée half the beans with enough of the beer to make a thick sauce.

4. Pour the puréed beans and reserved whole beans into the pan and cook over a high heat, scraping up the bottom so that it doesn't burn and stick, until the beans have cooked into a thick paste, adding a little extra beer as needed. Season with salt and pepper.

S E R V E S   6 – 8

450g/1lb pinto (or pinquito, or pink) or black beans, picked over	250–375g/9–13oz smoky bacon
2 medium onions, chopped	several mint leaves
1 head of garlic, unpeeled and cut into halves crosswise	salt

1. Soak beans overnight. Alternatively, place the beans in a saucepan with cold water to cover. Bring to the boil, cook for a few minutes, then remove from the heat. Leave to sit, covered, for 1 hour. The beans should have plumped up and softened somewhat, absorbing quite a bit of water in the process.

2. Add the onion, garlic, bacon, and mint to the pan and add water to cover.

3. Bring to the boil then reduce the heat to low and simmer uncovered, stirring once or twice, for 1½–2 hours, or until the beans are softened.

4. Add salt to taste.

NUTRITIONAL INFORMATION

	TOTAL FAT	SAT FAT	CHOL	ENERGY
Total	27g	9g	45mg	1969kcals/8355kJ
Serves 6	4.5g	1.5g	8mg	328kcals/1392kJ
Serves 8	3g	1g	6mg	246kcals/1044kJ

NUTRITIONAL INFORMATION

	TOTAL FAT	SAT FAT	CHOL	ENERGY
Total	38g	13g	68mg	2350kcals/9956kJ
Serves 6	6g	2g	11mg	392kcals/1659kJ
Serves 8	4.5g	1.5g	8mg	294kcals/1244kJ

SALSAS AND SPICE MIXTURES

Salsas are the gastronomical soul of Mexican food. The simplest dish – a bowl of rice, a boiled egg or a chunk of fish – is elevated to superb by the addition of a zesty, chilli-spiced salsa. Salsa can be as simple as chopped tomatoes, onions and chillies. One of the most breathtakingly delicious salsas I ever tasted was chopped coriander and green chillies, enlivened with a bit of garlic and a squirt of lime. Fresh fruit makes a refreshing salsa, its sweet, juicy flavour a balance for the fiery chilli pepper. Proprietary brands of salsa can be excellent; the best are from Mexico. I am fond of El Yucateca and Bufala Brand Chipotle salsa.

SALSA CRUDA

UNCOOKED SALSA
WITH GARLIC AND TOMATO

This is a classic salsa, rich with garlic, parsley and coriander. For a chunky salsa leave it as it is; for a smooth purée, give it a whirl in the blender for a moment.
Enjoy dabbed on to nearly anything, even just a swipe on a fresh corn tortilla or a spoonful alongside a bowl of rice.

SERVES 4

3 cloves garlic, chopped

2 jalapeño or serrano chillies, chopped

½ onion, chopped

450g/1lb flavourful raw tomatoes, chopped

2–3tbsp chopped fresh parsley

2–3tbsp chopped fresh coriander

salt and ground cumin to taste

juice of 1 lime

1. Combine all the ingredients and taste for seasoning. Keeps 4–5 days in the refrigerator.

NUTRITIONAL INFORMATION				
	TOTAL FAT	SAT FAT	CHOL	ENERGY
Total	1.5g	0.5g	0mg	108kcals/462kJ
Per Serving	0.4g	0.1g	0mg	27kcals/115kJ

SALSA FRIA

HOT TOMATO SALSA
WITH VINEGAR

SERVES 4

225g/8oz chunky tomato juice (use either crushed fresh ripe tomatoes or tinned tomatoes coarsely chopped, and their juice)

1 spring onion, thinly sliced

3–5 or more very hot small thin chillies such as cayenne or Thai

1 clove garlic, chopped

60–90ml/2–3fl oz water

large pinch of oregano

large pinch of ground cumin or crushed toasted cumin seeds

salt

30–45ml/2–3tbsp vinegar

small pinch of sugar (optional)

1. Combine all ingredients and leave to rest for at least 30 minutes to develop the flavours. Keeps up to 1 week in the refrigerator.

NUTRITIONAL INFORMATION				
	TOTAL FAT	SAT FAT	CHOL	ENERGY
Total	0.38g	0.01g	0mg	57kcals/245kJ
Per Serving	0.09g	0g	0mg	14kcals/61kJ

PINEAPPLE SALSA

SERVES 4

175–250ml/6–8fl oz
pineapple juice

1 clove garlic, chopped

1 spring onion, thinly sliced

1 ripe tomato, finely
chopped, or 50ml/2fl oz
tinned tomato juice or
crushed tomatoes

1tbsp coarsely chopped fresh
mint

1tbsp coarsely chopped
coriander

hot pepper sauce such as
Tabasco to taste, or crush a
fresh red chilli in a mortar
and pestle

pinch of ground cumin

juice of ½ lime plus a little of
the grated zest

salt

pinch of sugar

1. Mix the ingredients and leave to rest for at least 30 minutes to develop the flavours.

NUTRITIONAL INFORMATION				
	TOTAL FAT	SAT FAT	CHOL	ENERGY
Total	0.5g	0.1g	0mg	125kcals/538kJ
Per Serving	0.15g	0.02g	0mg	31kcals/135kJ

CHIPOTLE-ONION SALSA RELISH

SERVES 4

1 chipotle en adobo, plus
1tbsp of its marinade (from
can) or 2 dried chipotle
chillies softened with boiling
water and left to sit for
30 minutes

2–3 cloves garlic, chopped

1tbsp vegetable oil

1tsp chopped fresh coriander

juice of ½ lemon or lime

pinch of allspice or cloves

salt

1. Chop the chipotle chilli and combine with the onion, garlic, oil and coriander.
2. Season to taste with lemon or lime, allspice or cloves, and salt. Lasts up to 5 days in the refrigerator.

NUTRITIONAL INFORMATION				
	TOTAL FAT	SAT FAT	CHOL	ENERGY
Total	21g	3g	0mg	219kcals/903kJ
Per Serving	5.5g	0.75g	0mg	55kcals/226kJ

TOMATILLO SALSA

This is the basic green salsa, tangy from the slightly sour, fresh-tasting husk tomato, that you will find on tables throughout Mexico and parts of America's Southwest. It is especially good with rich foods such as pork carnitas, or bean and cheese burritos.

SERVES 4

400g/14oz tomatillos,
cooked, drained and puréed

1 onion, chopped

2 cloves garlic, chopped

2 fresh green chillies,
chopped, or to taste

2tbsp chopped fresh
coriander

salt and ground cumin to
taste

1. Combine all the ingredients and taste for seasoning. Lasts for up to 5 days in the refrigerator.

VARIATION
SALSA VERDE CON NOPALES

Add 175g/6oz cooked drained diced cactus (fresh or canned).

TIME-SAVING VARIATION

Combine 175g/6oz cooked, drained, diced cactus with approximately 100ml/4fl oz purchased salsa verde. Season to taste with salt, pepper, garlic, cumin and chopped coriander.

NUTRITIONAL INFORMATION				
	TOTAL FAT	SAT FAT	CHOL	ENERGY
Total	0.7g	0.01g	0mg	96kcals/409kJ
Per Serving	0.2g	0.0g	0mg	24kcals/102kJ

SALSA DE CHILE PASILLA

MILD RED CHILLI SAUCE

This is the classic red chilli sauce for making enchiladas, or simmering meats, or oomphing up soups or braises. You can omit the tomatoes if you like, or use stock for soaking the chillies for a richer-flavoured sauce.

Add this sauce to browned beef or pork as the braising liquid and simmer until tender for an excellent chilli rojo con carne, to spoon up in bowlfuls or wrap into tender tortillas for burritos and tacos.

SERVES 4

4 large smooth-skinned dried chillies

2–3 large crinkly chillies such as ancho, negro, pasilla, etc

475ml/16fl oz water or stock, hot but not boiling

6 cloves garlic, unpeeled

1 onion, peeled and cut into chunks

1 clove garlic, chopped

8 ripe tomatoes, quartered, or 400g/14oz canned tomatoes

¼tsp ground cumin

pinch of ground cinnamon

pinch of dried thyme

2–3tsp sugar

salt

15ml/1tbsp vegetable oil

juice of ½ lime, or to taste

1. Lightly toast the chillies over an open flame or in an ungreased heavy-based frying pan until they change colour.

2. Remove the stems, seeds and veins from the chillies, break the flesh up into little pieces and place in a bowl or saucepan. Pour in the water or stock to cover the chillies and leave, covered, to soften, about 20 minutes. The liquid should be cool enough to touch and the chillies softened and fleshy.

3. Meanwhile, roast the whole garlic cloves and onion chunks in an ungreased pan until lightly charred and the garlic is tender. Remove from the heat. When cool enough to handle, peel the garlic.

4. Chop the garlic and onion and place in a food processor or blender along with the raw chopped garlic, tomatoes, chillies, and enough of the soaking liquid to make a smoothish sauce. When the sauce is smooth whirl in the rest of the soaking liquid and season with cumin, cinnamon, thyme, sugar, and salt. (The sauce may be sieved for a smoother, more digestible texture.)

5. Heat the vegetable oil in a heavy-based pan. When hot, ladle in about half of the chilli sauce, cook down for a few minutes then ladle in the rest. Cook for about 10 minutes, or until the sauce thickens a little and concentrates its flavour.

6. Remove from the heat and season with lime, balancing it with the spices, salt and sugar. Lasts up to 1 week in the refrigerator.

NUTRITIONAL INFORMATION				
	TOTAL FAT	SAT FAT	CHOL	ENERGY
Total	13.5g	2g	0mg	323kcals/1362kJ
Per Serving	3.5g	0.5g	0mg	81kcals/341kJ

VARIATIONS

All mild chilli sauces can be prepared this way. Chillies such as ancho, negro, mulatto, and some pasillas will give a dark, almost chocolatey sauce; light red chillies such as New Mexico, California, guajillo, and some pasillas will give a brighter, lighter red sauce with a brighter, lighter flavour.

SALSA RANCHERA
COOKED TOMATO SAUCE

This all-purpose tomato and pepper sauce can be used to top eggs for huevos rancheros, served with grilled fish and plantains, thinned with stock for soup. The recipe makes about 2l/3½pt and keeps in the refrigerator for up to a week or in the freezer for up to 2 months (although it will pale when heated and needs to be spiced up with chilli pepper upon defrosting.

MAKES 2 L / 3 ½ P T

2tsp cumin seeds

1.5kg/3lb fresh or canned tomatoes, diced

85ml/3fl oz vegetable oil

2–3 small to medium-sized onions, peeled and chopped

4–6 cloves garlic, chopped

1tbsp dried oregano, crumbled

2–3 small hot dried chillies, crumbled, or 1 large mild green chilli, roasted, skinned and diced

1 green pepper, roasted, skinned and diced

salt

2–4tbsp chopped fresh coriander (optional)

1. Toast the cumin seeds in an ungreased heavy-based pan until fragrant, then crush coarsely. Set aside.

2. Purée the tomatoes and set aside.

3. Fry the onions and garlic until softened, then add the cumin seeds, oregano, chillies, green pepper and puréed tomatoes.

4. Simmer, stirring often, for about 45 minutes or until the sauce is richly flavoured and thickened. Season with salt to taste and add coriander if desired.

NUTRITIONAL INFORMATION				
	TOTAL FAT	SAT FAT	CHOL	ENERGY
Total	92g	11g	0mg	907kcals/3738kJ

SALSA DE MUCHOS CHILES Y JITOMATE

SALSA OF ROASTED TOMATOES
AND MANY DIFFERENT DRIED RED CHILLIES

This salsa bursts with quintessential Mexican flavours and while the tomatoes need to be roasted, the chillies toasted and ground, it is very simple to make.

Serve salsa de mucho chillies with anything cooked over an open fire or barbecue, as well as with simmered meals such as puchero. It is excellent on tortillas, with just about anything rolled up in them.

If you do not have each type of chilli, either omit or substitute: a New Mexico or California smooth-skinned red chilli could take the place of the guajilla and puya, for example.

SERVES 4

1 cascabel chilli	5 ripe red tomatoes, toasted to char evenly on all sides, then cooled
1 dry (not marinated) chipotle chilli	1–2 cloves garlic, chopped
1 guajillo chilli	100ml/4fl oz water
1 puya chilli	salt

1. Lightly toast the chillies on an ungreased pan until they lighten in colour and slightly puff up.

2. Cool and remove the stems, seeds and veins. Grind the flesh in a coffee grinder to a coarse powder.

3. Cut the tomatoes into pieces and purée with the garlic, chilli powder and water. Add salt to taste. Lasts up to 5 days in the refrigerator.

NUTRITIONAL INFORMATION				
	TOTAL FAT	SAT FAT	CHOL	ENERGY
Total	1.5g	0.5g	0mg	82kcals/352kJ
Per Serving	0.4g	0.1g	0mg	21kcals/88kJ

RECADO ROJO

RED CHILLI–CITRUS PASTE

This is an excellent all-purpose seasoning paste. Since it keeps for up to 2 weeks in the refrigerator and freezes up to 2 months, I tend to make a double batch so that I have it ready and on hand.

MAKES 50–85ML/2–3FL OZ

2 ancho chillies	pinch of grated orange zest
1 New Mexican or California chilli	15ml/1tbsp lemon or lime juice
1tsp cumin seeds	pinch of oregano
3 chopped cloves garlic	salt
30ml/2tbsp fresh orange juice	

1. Remove the stems and seeds from the chillies then tear the flesh up into smallish pieces.

2. Lightly toast in an ungreased heavy-based pan until the chillies change colour slightly. Do not allow them to burn.

3. Lightly toast the cumin seeds in an ungreased heavy-based pan until they are fragrant and slightly darkened.

4. Grind the chillies and cumin together in a spice grinder, coffee grinder or food processor until they form a rough, mealy consistency.

5. Combine with the garlic, orange juice and zest, lemon or lime juice and oregano and purée in a food processor or blender until a smoothish paste is formed. Season with salt to taste.

TIME-SAVING VARIATION

Instead of whole chillies, use 2tbsp each ancho and pastilla or New Mexico chilli powder. Instead of whole cumin seeds, use ground cumin. Toast both as indicated in the recipe, though it will take only a few seconds as they are already ground.

NUTRITIONAL INFORMATION				
	TOTAL FAT	SAT FAT	CHOL	ENERGY
Total	0.5g	0.03g	0mg	23kcals/97kJ

SALSA VERDE DE TOMATILLO Y CHILLI ROJO

GREEN SALSA
WITH RED DRIED CHILLI

This tomatillo salsa is especially good with simmered chicken or pork, a pile of warm tortillas alongside, although it goes well with grilled seafood, too.

SERVES 4

½ each: dry chipotle chilli, guajillo, cascabel, and puya

1 clove garlic, chopped

400g/14oz tomatillos, cooked, coarsely chopped or puréed

2tbsp vinegar or to taste

salt to taste

pinch of ground cumin (optional)

pinch of ground turmeric (optional)

1. Lightly toast the chillies until they change in colour, about 5 minutes. Remove the stems and seeds and grind the flesh in a coffee grinder.

2. Combine with the garlic, tomatillos and vinegar, then season to taste with salt, cumin and turmeric. Lasts up to 5 days in the refrigerator.

NUTRITIONAL INFORMATION				
	TOTAL FAT	SAT FAT	CHOL	ENERGY
Total	0.5g	0g	0mg	71kcals/306kJ
Per Serving	0.1g	0g	0mg	18kcals/76kJ

SALSA DE LIMON Y CILANTRO

CORIANDER AND LIME SALSA

This hot and tangy purée of green coriander, chillies and lime is a basic in my kitchen.

SERVES 4

50g/2oz fresh coriander, chopped

1–2 green chillies, or more, chopped

juice of 1 lime

3 cloves garlic, chopped

1–2 ripe tomatoes, chopped

½tsp ground cumin

salt

1. Combine all the ingredients. Lasts 5–7 days in the refrigerator.

NUTRITIONAL INFORMATION				
	TOTAL FAT	SAT FAT	CHOL	ENERGY
Total	0.5g	0.01g	0mg	24kcals/99kJ
Per Serving	0.1g	0g	0mg	6kcals/25kJ

ACHIOTE SEASONING

Also called annatto, these small rock-hard seeds have a lemony, almost saffron-scented aroma and flavour, and the ability to colour almost anything a bright yellow (achiote is used to dye margarine and butter).

Achiote may be ground dry in a coffee or spice grinder, or simmered in water to cover until softened then pounded flat in a mortar and pestle or pureed in a blender or food processor.

GROUND ACHIOTE

4tbsp achiote seeds

1. Place in a clean spice or coffee grinder and whirl until a fine powder is formed.

SIMMERED ACHIOTE

Place achiote seeds in a small saucepan with water to cover. Bring to the boil, then reduce the heat and simmer for 30–40 minutes. Leave to rest overnight, then grind or purée with only just enough liquid to bind it.

Achiote paste may be stored in the freezer for up to 6 months.

ACHIOTE OIL

Heat 3 tbsp achiote seeds in 85–120ml/3–4fl oz vegetable oil only until bubbles form around the edge of the saucepan. Leave to infuse overnight, then strain and discard the seeds. The resulting oil will be yellow-tinted.

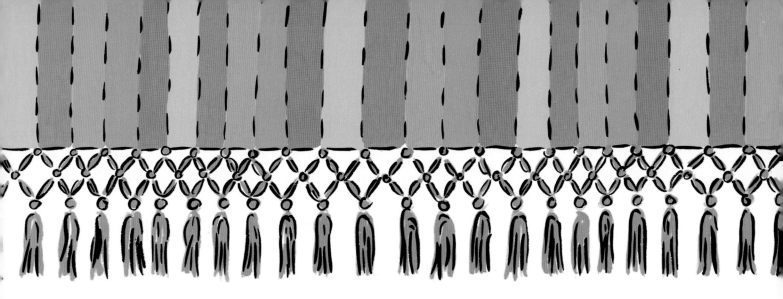

CHAPTER TWO

SIMMERED MEATS, BROTHS AND TAMALES

★ ★ ★ ★ ★

SIMMERED MEATS, THEIR BROTHS, AND DISHES TO MAKE FROM THEM

A pot of simmering meat or poultry and stock forms the basis of the Mexican kitchen. Many meals begin with soup, then progress to the meat that has simmered in the pot. This is important in a country where poverty is endemic. I've heard it said that roasting is "for the rich! You only get one meal from the pot".

CALDO DE POLLO

CHICKEN STOCK

Instead of using a whole chicken, you can use inexpensive cuts such as wings, necks or legs.
Simmering chicken with vegetables makes a good flavourful stock to use in other sauces, soups and stews. It also yields tender moist meat for moles, enchiladas and so forth.

MAKES 2L/4PT

1 chicken, cut into serving parts	2 stock cubes
3–4 carrots, sliced	several sprigs fresh coriander, chopped
2 onions, chopped	salt and pepper
3–4 cloves garlic, peeled and chopped	

1. Place the chicken, carrots, onions and garlic in a large pot and fill with water.
2. Bring to the boil. Skim off any scum that develops on the surface as it comes to the boil, then reduce the heat and add the stock cubes and coriander.
3. Simmer covered over a low heat for 1½–2 hours or until the chicken is tender and the stock flavourful.
4. Remove the chicken from the stock and serve as desired.

CALDO DE PUERCO

SIMMERED PORK
AND ITS STOCK

SERVES 4

1.5–1.75kg/3–4lb pork, cut into cubes, or 1.75–2.25kg/4–5lb country-style pork spare ribs	1tsp ground cumin
	1tsp ground coriander
	1tsp dried oregano
1 onion, chopped	2 bay leaves
2l/4pt water	1–2 chicken stock cubes
3 cloves garlic, coarsely chopped	salt and pepper to taste

1. Place the pork, onion and half the garlic in a large pot of water and bring to the boil. Skim off the scum that forms, then reduce the heat.
2. Add the stock cubes. For light stock and meat that is to be cooked a second time, simmer for only 45–60 minutes. For tender meat and rich stock, simmer for about 3 hours.

NUTRITIONAL INFORMATION				
	TOTAL FAT	SAT FAT	CHOL	ENERGY
Total	142g	50g	1380mg	2981kcals/12472kJ
Per Serving	35.5g	12.5g	345mg	745kcals/3118kJ

PAVO EN MOLE POBLANO

TURKEY

WITH MOLE SAUCE

The word "mole" comes from the Aztec *molli*, meaning "to grind", and mole sauces, of which there are a near-endless variety, are made from finely ground ingredients, simmered first into a thick paste then thinned and simmered into a glossy smooth sauce. Mole makes a sumptuous filling for tacos, tostadas, enchiladas and tortillas. This recipe makes a huge potful of mole paste. Since mole improves by making ahead of time it is a marvellous dish for guests, and it freezes beautifully.

½ turkey or 1 chicken, cut into serving pieces

3 bay leaves

1–2 onions, chopped

5 cloves garlic, chopped

3 carrots, diced

handful of fresh coriander

handful of parsley

2–3 chicken stock cubes

MOLE

6–8 ancho chillies

3 mulatto or chillies negro

2–3 pasilla or smooth red chillies such as New Mexico or California

¼tsp coriander seeds

⅛tsp black peppercorns

2.5cm/1in cinnamon stick

6–8 cloves, the aromatic round part at the head only

½tsp fennel seeds or anise

150g/5oz sesame seeds

450g/1lb tomatoes, preferably small flavourful ones

5–8 cloves garlic, unpeeled and whole

1 large onion

65–90g/2½–3½oz raisins

75–90ml/5–6tbsp olive oil or lard

65g/2½oz almonds

100g/4oz pumpkin seeds

25g/1oz peanuts

2 fat slices of French or country bread (about 50–75g/2–3oz), cut into bite-sized cubes

2 stale tortillas, cut into strips or bite-sized pieces

60–90ml/4–6tbsp red or white wine vinegar

40g/1½oz plain chocolate

475–750ml/16–24fl oz chicken stock, or as needed

salt and pepper to taste

TO SERVE

warmed tortillas

chopped spring onions and/or chopped fresh coriander

thinly sliced cabbage

soured cream (optional)

lime wedges

1. Combine the turkey or chicken with the bay leaves, onions, garlic and carrots, in a huge pot and fill it with water. Bring to the boil, then skim off the scum that forms at the top.

2. Add coriander, parsley and stock cubes and reduce the heat, then simmer, covered, for about 3 hours or until the broth is flavourful and the meat very tender. Set aside. Use this stock (caldo de guajalote), for the mole, and also for soups.

3. Meanwhile, make the mole. Lightly toast the chillies on an ungreased frying pan until they change colour slightly.

4. Tear the chillies into pieces then place in a bowl and cover with boiling water. Cover the bowl and leave to soften for about 20 minutes, turning once or twice to be sure they are evenly soaked.

5. Lightly toast the coriander seeds, peppercorns, cinnamon stick, cloves, fennel seeds or anise and about two-thirds of the sesame seeds in the frying pan. When fragrant, remove to a spice or coffee grinder and whirl to grind. Remove any pieces of hard, large spices such as cinnamon that are left. Set the spice mixture aside.

6. Grill the tomatoes, garlic and onion until charred on the outside and softened inside. Set aside. When cool dice the tomatoes and onions, then remove the garlic skins and chop the garlic flesh.

7. Fry the raisins in 15ml/1tbsp of oil until they plump up. Set aside.

8. In the same pan, toast the almonds, pumpkin seeds and peanuts, cooking until the pumpkin seeds sputter and pop. Remove from the heat, then grind in the spice or coffee grinder. Set aside.

9. Add 15–30ml/1–2tbsp of oil to the pan and lightly brown the bread and tortillas. Remove from the heat and set aside.

10. Remove the stems and seeds from the soaked chillies and purée with half the charred tomatoes, onion and garlic in a blender or food processor.

11. Heat 30ml/2tbsp oil in a frying pan then ladle the chilli-tomato mixture into it. Cook over medium heat until concentrated and paste-like.

12. In a blender or food processor, purée the remaining tomatoes, onions and garlic with the ground seeds and the spice mixture and nuts, raisins and toasted bread and tortillas, whirling until smooth and sauce-like, adding stock as needed to keep it thin enough to be smooth.

13. Combine the two mixtures in a saucepan. Add the vinegar and stir in the chocolate. Simmer for about 20 minutes, adding more stock as needed. The final result should be a rich, spicy paste.

14. Season with salt, pepper, cinnamon, and vinegar to taste.

15. To serve, thin the mole paste with warm stock until it reaches the desired consistency. Warm turkey in remaining oil; warm, too, a stack of corn tortillas. Serve the warm turkey blanketed with the mole sauce, sprinkled with remaining sesame seeds and spring onions and/or coriander, accompanied by a stack of warm corn tortillas, cabbage, and soured cream.

VARIATIONS
MOLE TACOS

Prepare tortillas, preferably fresh. Heat 3–4 tbsp mole dissolved in 175–250ml/6–8fl oz chicken stock and simmer until thick and sauce-like. Spoon on to tortillas, then top with shredded cabbage, coriander, chopped onion and garlic with soured cream or fromage frais.

ENCHILADAS DE MOLE ROJO
Recipe on page 38.

BARBECUED DUCK BREASTS WITH MOLE

Serve skinless grilled duck breast, slightly charred on the outside, rare inside with a puddle of warm simmered mole. Sprinkle with toasted sesame seeds, pickled jalapeños, chopped spring onions, and offer warm tortillas. For an exotic garnish, strew the duck and mole with unsprayed rose petals.

NUTRITIONAL INFORMATION			
	TOTAL FAT	SAT FAT	CHOL	ENERGY
Total	323g	57g	633mg	5133kcals/21424kJ

TIME-SAVING VARIATION

Use chilli powder(s), preferably homemade from individual chillies, instead of whole chillies and peanut butter in place of the various nuts. Bread may be omitted, and tortilla chips used in place of fried tortilla strips.

CALDO DEL RES
BEEF STOCK AND MEAT

This makes a light stock, good for soups and casseroles; it yields a pot of tender meats for tacos and so forth.

MAKES 2L/4PT STOCK

1kg/2lb beef chuck, flank steak, or brisket per 1–2 litres of cold water

0.5–1kg/1–2lb oxtails

8 cloves garlic, coarsely chopped

2 onions, coarsely chopped

1 bay leaf

1 stick celery, including leaves

pinch of cloves

1tsp dried thyme

1tsp dried oregano

salt and pepper

2¼pt cold water

2 beef stock cubes (optional)

1. Combine the beef, oxtails, garlic, onion, bay leaf, celery, cloves, thyme, oregano, salt and pepper in a large pot and fill with cold water.

2. Bring to the boil, skimming off all the while the grey scum that forms on the top of the pot.

3. Reduce the heat to a slow simmer, add the stock cubes if using, and cook the meat, covered, for 3 hours, or until the meat is very tender and the stock full-flavoured.

NUTRITIONAL INFORMATION			
	TOTAL FAT	SAT FAT	CHOL	ENERGY
Total	255g	115g	1303mg	5921kcals/24747kJ

VARIATION
BROWN STOCK

Sear the meat in a little oil before simmering it with water and herbs.

ROPA VIEJA

OLD CLOTHES IN TATTERS

The pungent garnish of coriander is lovely on this rich, meaty dish; for variety, garnish the meat with fresh mint or watercress instead.

SERVES 4

2 onions, chopped

5 cloves garlic, chopped

15–30ml/1–2tbsp oil, or as needed

450–900g/1–2lb flank steak from Caldo de Res (page 23), shredded with two forks or your fingers

5 ripe tomatoes or 350g/12oz canned, diced

pinch of sugar

salt

⅛–¼tsp ground cumin

⅛–¼tsp ground cinnamon

pinch of allspice

1–2tsp mild chilli powder

1 marinated chipotle chilli, diced, plus 5–10ml/1–2tsp of the marinade

¼tsp dried oregano

a few drops of vinegar

3tbsp chopped fresh coriander

¼ cabbage, thinly sliced, dressed with 1tsp each of olive oil and vinegar

1. Fry the onions and garlic in the oil until softened then add the meat and brown for a few minutes.

2. Add the tomatoes, sugar, salt, cumin, cinnamon, allspice, chilli powder, chipotle chilli and marinade, and oregano. Cook over low to medium heat until the meat is richly browned in a small amount of thick sauce.

3. Serve hot, sprinkled with coriander and cabbage.

NUTRITIONAL INFORMATION			
	TOTAL FAT	SAT FAT	CHOL	ENERGY
Total	173g	73g	683mg	2824kcals/11786kJ
Per Serving	43g	18g	171mg	706kcals/2946kJ

CARNE MACHACA

SHREDDED BEEF
WITH SEASONING

SERVES 4

1 onion, diced

3 cloves garlic, chopped

15ml/1tbsp vegetable oil

450–900g/1–2lb tender simmered beef from Caldo del Res (page 23), shredded with two forks

3 ripe tomatoes, diced

2 large mild green chillies such as poblano or Anaheim, roasted, peeled and diced, or 2 green peppers and 2 medium-sized green chillies such as jalapeño, all roasted, peeled and diced

½tsp crushed dried oregano

½tsp ground cumin

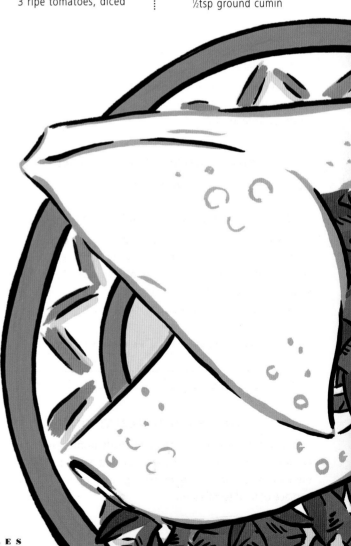

1. Lightly fry the onion and garlic in the oil until softened.

2. Add the meat, tomatoes, chillies, oregano and cumin and continue to cook for about 15 minutes, adding a little Caldo del Res stock now and again to keep the meat from becoming too dry.

3. Serve as a filling for tacos, etc, or heaped on to a plate surrounded by beans, rice, salsa and salad.

NUTRITIONAL INFORMATION				
	TOTAL FAT	SAT FAT	CHOL	ENERGY
Total	172g	73g	683mg	2705kcals/11283kJ
Per Serving	43g	18g	171mg	676kcals/2821kJ

COCIDO

SIMMERED DISH OF MEAT, VEGETABLES AND FRUIT

A cocido is a simmered dinner, much like the puchero of Spain, pot au feu of France, and bollito misto of Italy. From one pot you have a rich stock to eat as a soup course. The second course yields a variety of meats and vegetables: serve on a platter along with boiled potatoes, and several salsas (choose from the Salsa chapter).

Because of its abundance, a cocido is a dish you make in a huge pot: throughout the coming week you will have the basis for many homey, flavourful meals that can be put together almost instantly.

This particular cocido makes a stock that is spicy from chilli and chorizo, yet slightly sweet and fragrant from the fruit. Other vegetables may be added to the pot: par-boiled potatoes or sweet potatoes, hunks of corn on the cob, strips of sweet red pepper, yellow summer squash.

SERVES 6 - 8

900g/2lb boneless pork, either in one chunk or bite-sized pieces

2 bay leaves

1 onion, chopped

3 cloves garlic, chopped

2tbsp chopped fresh coriander

1 carrot, thinly sliced

2 sticks celery, diced

2 chicken stock cubes

½ chorizo (75–100g/3–4oz), cut into 2–3 pieces

1 poussin or ½ chicken, cut into serving or half-serving pieces

4–5 tomatoes, chopped

½–1 guajillo chilli, soaked and puréed, or 1–2tsp coarsely ground toasted guajillo or other mild chilli powder

grated zest of ¼–½ orange

juice of 3 oranges

1 courgette, cut into bite-sized pieces

¼ cabbage, thinly sliced and blanched

1 apple, cut into bite-sized pieces

10 prunes, pitted

¼tsp ground cinnamon

pinch of dried ginger

salt

1. Combine the pork, bay leaves, onion, garlic, coriander, carrot and celery in a large pot and fill with water.

2. Bring to the boil then reduce the heat and simmer over a low heat. Skim the scum that forms when mixture boils first time, but leave any subsequent scum.

3. Add the stock cubes and cook for 1 hour or until the meat is becoming tender, then add the chorizo, chicken, tomatoes, chilli, cumin and orange zest. Continue to cook for another 30 minutes and skim off the fat that forms at the surface.

4. Add the orange juice, courgette, cabbage, apple, prunes, cinnamon and ginger and continue to simmer for another 15 minutes or until the courgette is tender.

5. Season with salt and serve in two courses: with tender boiled noodles or rice for a first course and with boiled potatoes for a second course. Accompany with Salsa de Muchos Chillies y Jitomate (page 18) or other fresh salsa to taste.

NUTRITIONAL INFORMATION				
	TOTAL FAT	SAT FAT	CHOL	ENERGY
Total	112g	39g	990mg	2689kcals/11283kJ
Per Serving (6)	18g	6.5g	165mg	448kcals/1880kJ
Per Serving (8)	14g	5g	124mg	336kcals/1410kJ

MOCHOMOS

SHREDDED PORK
WITH GUACAMOLE

SERVES 4

900g/2lb very tender cooked pork

vegetable oil

salt and pepper

TO GARNISH

guacamole

shredded lettuce

2tbsp chopped fresh coriander

2tbsp chopped onion

cherry tomatoes or other strong-flavoured tomatoes, chopped

fresh salsa

1. Shred the meat into fine strips, then brown in a small amount of oil if needed. Season well with salt and pepper.

2. Serve the hot meat garnished with guacamole, shredded lettuce, coriander, onion, and tomatoes and offer fresh salsa as desired.

NUTRITIONAL INFORMATION			
	TOTAL FAT	SAT FAT	CHOL	ENERGY
Total	91g	23g	760mg	1885kcals/7889kJ
Per Serving	23g	5.5g	190mg	471kcals/1972kJ

PUERCO EN MOLE VERDE

PORK

IN GREEN CHILLI SAUCE

Pork in green mole is one of Mexico's great classics (and simple to prepare as well). Pork cooked in stock until just tender is then simmered in tomatillo sauce. The tart tomatillos counteract the richness of the pork.

SERVES 4

2 cloves garlic, chopped	250ml/8fl oz pork stock from Caldo de Puerco (page 21)
450g/1lb cooked, drained tomatillos, puréed	1kg/2lb pork from Caldo de Puerco
3–4 serrano chillies or 2–3 jalapeño chillies, chopped	2–3tbsp mixed chopped fresh herbs: parsley, watercress, coriander, and purslane, if available
45ml/3tbsp oil	

1. In a blender or food processor, purée the garlic with the tomatillos and chillies.

2. Heat the oil in a pan and pour the tomatillo mixture in. Cook over a medium high heat for about 10 minutes or until thickened.

3. Add the stock and meat and continue to simmer for 1–1½ hours or until the meat is tender.

4. Serve sprinkled with chopped fresh herbs.

NUTRITIONAL INFORMATION			
	TOTAL FAT	SAT FAT	CHOL	ENERGY
Total	164.5g	52.5g	1380mg	3265kcals/13655kJ
Per Serving	41g	13g	345mg	816kcals/3414kJ

CARNITAS

CRISPY TENDER PORK

SERVES 4

1.5–1.75kg/3–4lb pork, use a cut such as a shoulder that has its bone in place and a bit of fat in the meat	1tsp ground cumin
	1tsp ground coriander
	1tsp dried oregano
1 onion, chopped	2 bay leaves
3 cloves garlic, coarsely chopped	1–2 chicken stock cubes
	salt and pepper to taste

1. Prepare pork as in Caldo de Puerco (page 21). As an optional seasoning, add ½ chopped chilli chipotle to the simmering stock.

2. Place the meat in a large roasting pan. Season with salt and pepper and bake, uncovered, in a preheated oven at 230°C/450°F/Gas Mark 8 until sizzling and browned, 20–30 minutes. Pull chunks of meat off the bone and shred with two forks. Discard the fat and serve meat warm, with a selection of salsas. Tortillas, rice and beans round out the meal authentically.

TAMALES

A good tamale is memorable: tender steamed masa dough, slightly mealy, moist yet never gummy. It should taste of stoneground corn and antiquity.

A tamale may be filled with nearly any sort of savoury or sweet filling: meat or poultry in mole; vegetables in pipian; seafood in red chilli paste; pineapple and brown sugar; or cheese and green chillies. Alternatively, it may be left unfilled, traditional in many regions as an accompaniment for celebratory feasts.

An unfilled tamale may have bits of vegetables beaten into the masa: kernels of sweetcorn are delicious; so, too, are bits of golden squash flowers or enough simmered black beans to stud the dough like little grey-black dots.

Lard is the traditional fat used in making tamales. It needs to be whipped until fluffy and light, then the masa is beaten in, and slowly, very slowly, enough warm stock to make a light dough. I have experimented using both butter and oil as substitutes for lard. The results are not as fine as the lard-based traditional method, but nice enough for me to want to make them again.

TAMALES

SERVES 6

TAMALE DOUGH	FILLING
about 20 dried corn husks	shredded beef or pork seasoned with mole or any sauce of red chillies, Picadillo (page 66), or any chilli-seasoned meat, chicken or fish
225g/8oz masa harina	
2tsp baking powder	
1½tsp salt	
85ml/3fl oz vegetable oil	
375ml/13fl oz lukewarm stock	

1. Place the corn husks in a bowl and pour boiling water over them. Leave to rest for at least 30 minutes or until the corn husks soften and become pliable. Remove from the water and wipe dry.

2. Combine the masa harina with the baking powder and salt. Stir to mix well, then whisk in the oil, letting the mixture form very light and fluffy grains.

3. Using a wooden spoon, stir in the stock, increasing the amount you add as you stir continuously. When the mixture forms a light dough it is ready.

4. To form the tamales, first lay out a pliable piece of corn husk and spread with masa dough, then lay one on each side and spread those, too, until you have a rectangle that is spread with masa dough, leaving 1cm/½in or so border around the edges..

5. Place 1–2tbsp of the filling in the centre of each, then fold over the sides, squeezing a bit to seal the masa dough and husks. Fold over the open ends and pile into a steamer. Repeat until the dough or corn husks are used up.

6. Steam over boiling water at a steady bubble for 1 hour. Remove from the steamer.

7. Eat right away, or reheat later by steaming for 30 minutes.

NUTRITIONAL INFORMATION				
	TOTAL FAT	SAT FAT	CHOL	ENERGY
Total	98g	11g	0mg	1729kcals/7176kJ
Per Serving	16.5g	2.0g	0mg	288kcals/1196kJ

TAMALE DE QUESO DE CABRITA

GOAT'S CHEESE AND ROASTED GREEN CHILLI TAMALES

SERVES 6

1 quantity of tamale dough and corn husks (page 28)

225g/8oz mild goat's cheese, such as Montrachet, cut into small chunks

2–3 roasted, peeled poblano chillies, lightly marinated in a little garlic, olive oil and lemon and cut into thin strips

1–2tbsp chopped fresh coriander

1. Spread out the dough as directed in the recipe on page 28 then place on it 1tbsp of goat's cheese, strips of chilli and a sprinkling of fresh coriander.

2. Close up and steam as on page 28. Serve hot.

NUTRITIONAL INFORMATION			
	TOTAL FAT	SAT FAT	CHOL	ENERGY
Total	143g	37.5g	0mg	2274kcals/9439kJ
Per Serving	24g	6.25g	0mg	379kcals/1573kJ

TAMALES DE PESCADO CON ENSALADA

FISH TAMALES

WITH WATERCRESS SALAD

Fish tamales are popular throughout Mexico. Instead of sea bass, prawns may be used.

SERVES 6

1 quantity tamale dough (page 28), using fish stock instead of chicken stock

20 corn husks as in above recipe or several banana leaves, cut into 30 × 30cm/12 × 12in pieces

FILLING

450g/1lb sea bass fillets or other white-fleshed fish, cut into bite-sized pieces

Red Chilli-Citrus Paste (page 18)

1tbsp chopped fresh coriander

watercress salad, dressed in olive oil and vinegar

1. Prepare the masa dough for tamales. Set aside.

2. Soak the corn husks (see page 28). Set aside to soften.

3. Combine the fish with the chilli paste and coriander.

4. Form the tamales as on page 28, using the fish filling. (If using banana leaves, make them pliable by heating over the flame gently for a moment or so, then filling and folding into an envelope shape.) Place the parcels in a steamer and cook over medium-high heat for about 40 minutes, adding more water to the steamer if needed to keep them from scorching.

5. Serve hot or leave to cool and heat as desired. Serve with watercress salad.

VARIATION

For a lighter version of the fish tamale, omit the dough entirely and simply wrap the chilli-seasoned fish chunks in the soaked corn husks or warmed banana leaves. Dab a bit of masa harina paste on the soaked corn husks to help them stick together, then steam. Serve with wedges of lime and fresh coriander.

NUTRITIONAL INFORMATION				
	TOTAL FAT	SAT FAT	CHOL	ENERGY
Total	102g	11.5g	230mg	2129kcals/8861kJ
Per Serving	17g	2.0g	38mg	355kcals/1477kJ

POSOLE

Posole (also spelled pozole) was eaten in pre-Columbian Mexico. It is no more than kernels of a specific type of corn, cooked in a solution of slaked lime to soften and swell them. The process pops off their skins, giving the plump corn a unique, earthy flavour and mealy yet chewy consistency. (This is the same corn preparation mashed into a dough and used for tortillas, tamales and grits.)

Posole is the quintessential Mexican comfort food, spooned up at a Mexican street-stall, a family celebration dinner, or a restaurant (many specialize in posole one day a week). Few other things in life put the world as right as does a bowl of posole.

Anything can be cooked into broth for posole. A large amount of sweet simmered garlic is traditional. So is half a pig's head (though authentic and delicious, it is a bit grisly – spareribs or similar cuts are excellent in its place). Other meats or poultry may be used instead of pork: beef, turkey, lamb, even duck.

SERVES 10-12

450–900g/1–2lb dried hominy, or several large cans canned hominy (preferably a combination of white and yellow)

450g/1lb lean stewing pork or beef

1–1½kg/2–3lb fattier pork meat such as spareribs (or beef, or lamb)

450g/1lb smoked pork shanks or hocks (optional)

2 beef stock cubes

2 chicken stock cubes

2 heads of garlic, unpeeled and unseparated, each cut into halves crosswise

2–3 onions, chopped

3 bay leaves

1 1–1½kg/2¼–3lb chicken

CONDIMENTS

1 onion, chopped

small bowl of fresh oregano leaves, for crumbling

1 cabbage, thinly sliced

1 bunch radishes, cut into julienne strips

2–3 limes, cut into wedges

1 bunch fresh coriander, chopped

fresh jalapeño peppers, chopped

1. If using dried hominy, soak in water to cover for 8 hours or overnight. Drain.

2. Place the soaked hominy in a large pot with water to cover and simmer for 2–3 hours or until tender. Taste as you go since some hominy cooks quicker than others. If using canned hominy, simply open the cans and drain.

3. Combine the meats, stock cubes, garlic, onions, bay leaves, and water to fill the pot.

4. Bring to the boil, reduce the heat to a low simmer, and spoon off any scum that forms at first on the surface. (After that, ignore any more scum – it will cook back into the stock).

5. Cook over a low heat for about 2 hours, then add the chicken. Continue to simmer for another 1½–2½ hours or until the meats are very tender, the chicken tender but not falling apart, and the broth very flavourful.

6. About 30 mins before the broth is ready, add the hominy.

7. Serve the posole in bowls: a few big spoonfuls of hominy, the rich broth, a chunk or two of the various meats and an array of condiments for each eater to add to his or her whim.

NUTRITIONAL INFORMATION				
	TOTAL FAT	SAT FAT	CHOL	ENERGY
Total	271g	130g	2235mg	6979kcals/29176kJ
Per Serving (10)	27g	13g	224mg	698kcals/2918kJ
Per Serving (12)	23g	11g	186mg	582kcals/2431kJ

POSOLE DE HONGOS

WILD MUSHROOM POSOLE

Unlike other posoles, this one is best when subtly spiced since the pairing of forest-scented mushrooms and earthy hominy is lovely. A tiny drop of your favourite fresh salsa is plenty. If using dried mushrooms, break them into small pieces when you combine them with the hot stock. Mushrooms with tough stems such as shiitakes should have their stems removed first and discarded.

SERVES 4 – 6

225g/8oz fresh flavourful mushrooms such as shiitake, porcini (cèpes), chanterelle or trompets de morte or a combination of dried ones combined with fresh cultivated ones (try 15–20 dried shiitakes plus 15g/½oz dried porcini and 100g/4oz fresh cultivated ones)

350–450g/12–16oz cooked, drained hominy (page 31)

a few drops to a few tbsp of your favourite salsa (depending on its strength)

salt and pepper

slices of Monterey Jack cheese (optional)

1. If using fresh mushrooms, combine with hot stock and bring to the boil. If using dried and cultivated combined, pour the hot stock over the dried and fresh mushrooms, cover and leave for 30 minutes.

2. Add the hominy and salsa. Simmer for another 15–25 minutes or until the flavours are melded.

3. Season with salt and pepper and serve right away, either as it is or ladled over a slab of cheese.

NUTRITIONAL INFORMATION				
	TOTAL FAT	SAT FAT	CHOL	ENERGY
Total	5.5g	0.5g	0mg	2098kcals/8776kJ
Per Serving (4)	1.5g	0.1g	0mg	524kcals/2194kJ
Per Serving (6)	1.0g	0.1g	0mg	350kcals/1463kJ

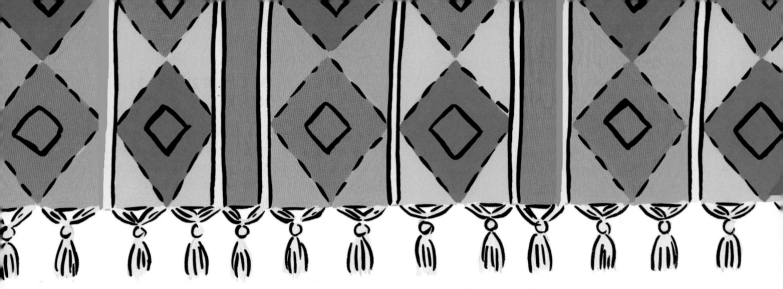

CHAPTER THREE

CASSEROLES, EGG DISHES AND VEGETARIAN MEALS

★ ★ ★ ★ ★

CAZUELAS

CASSEROLE DISHES

Everywhere you go in Mexico you see them: gaily painted rustic earthenware
casseroles, containing savoury mixtures of all sorts of things bubbling away.
Stuffed tortillas, tortillas layered with sauces, pasta and rice dishes – all are part of
the rich variety of main course on offer. The classic paella, a magnificent
casserole of rice and seafood, is included here, and a homey dish of fideos –
broth-cooked pasta.

CHILAQUILES CON POLLO

CHICKEN CHILAQUILES

Chilaquiles is a casserole of broken up tortillas – its name, in
fact, means broken up old sombreros – layered with spicy
sauce, meat or poultry, often with a cheesy topping. Soured
cream, fried chorizo or eggs – scrambled or fried – are often
part of the dish.
Chilaquiles are often made in marketplace cafés, crisp and firm
in the morning when they are put on sale, delectably mushy
late in the day as the tortillas begin to dissolve in the sauce. It's
hard to know which way they are more delicious.

SERVES 6

12 stale tortillas, cut into
strips

vegetable oil

1 small to medium chicken,
shredded or pulled apart into
small pieces

salt and pepper to taste

Mild Salsa Verde de Tomatillos
(page 15)

2 mint leaves

2tbsp chopped fresh
coriander

5 cloves garlic, chopped

¼tsp ground cumin

350g/12oz soured cream or
crème fraîche

350g/12oz white cheese such
as Mozzarella, Manchego or
Monterey Jack, coarsely
grated

100–175g/4–6oz Parmesan or
similar cheese such as
Pecorino Romano, grated

TO SERVE

3–4tbsp chopped fresh
coriander

1 onion, diced or sliced

2 hard-boiled eggs, sliced

thinly sliced chillies or salsa
as desired

1. Toss the tortilla strips lightly with a small amount of oil,
then arrange on a baking sheet. Bake in a preheated oven at
180°C/350°F/Gas Mark 4 until they are crisp and golden,
about 30 minutes. Check often; when crisp, remove and set
aside.
2. Arrange the chicken in a 23 × 33cm/9 × 13in or 30 ×
30cm/12 × 12in baking casserole then sprinkle with salt and
pepper and half the salsa verde, a leaf of mint and a sprinkling
of coriander, garlic and cumin, half the soured cream or crème
fraîche, and half the tortilla strips. Top with half the cheese,
then repeat until everything is used up, ending with a layer of
cheese.
3. Bake, covered, in the oven at 180°C/350°F/Gas Mark 4 for
35–40 minutes, then uncover and continue baking until the
cheese is lightly golden in spots.
4. Serve right away, garnished with coriander, onion, hard-
boiled egg and chillies or salsa.

NUTRITIONAL INFORMATION			
	TOTAL FAT	SAT FAT	CHOL	ENERGY
Total	270g	139g	1450mg	5351kcals/22417kJ
Per Serving	45g	23g	242mg	892kcals/3736kJ

VEGETARIAN VARIATION
Omit the chicken. Serve with black beans on the side.

PAPADZULES

YUCATECAN ENCHILADAS OF HARD-BOILED EGG AND PUMPKIN SEEDS

Topped with pickled onions, that quintessential Yucatecan relish, these enchiladas are filled with diced hard-boiled eggs and sauced with both a tomato and a ground pumpkin seed sauce.

SERVES 6

15 small or 8 medium tomatoes, lightly charred on an ungreased pan

2 small to medium onions, halved, lightly charred then peeled and chopped

1 onion, raw and chopped

10 cloves garlic, lightly charred in their peel then squeezed out

3 cloves garlic, raw and chopped

85ml/3fl oz olive oil

1½ Scots bonnet or chilli habañero, or 3 yellow guero chillies, chopped

salt

350ml/12fl oz chicken stock

½ head garlic, unpeeled

1tbsp chopped fresh coriander

225g/8oz pumpkin seeds, shelled but raw

12 tortillas

8–12 hard-boiled eggs, chopped

TO SERVE

pickled onions

1. In a blender or food processor, purée the charred tomatoes, charred onions, half the raw onions, the charred garlic and raw garlic. Heat 1tbsp of oil in a pan then add the tomato purée and half the chillies and cook until the mixture thickens and the oil separates. Season with salt and thin out with chicken stock until the mixture is a light tomato sauce consistency. Set aside.

2. Combine the remaining onion, remaining chillies, coriander and unpeeled garlic in a saucepan with the remaining chicken stock. Bring to the boil then reduce the heat and simmer until the garlic is tender.

3. Lightly toast the pumpkin seeds in a heavy frying pan carefully so that they do not burn – they will pop and sputter out of the pan. When toasted, place in a blender or food processor and grind until mealy, then add the simmered garlic and onion plus a little of the stock to the pumpkin seeds and purée until a paste forms. Stir in enough stock to thicken.

4. Warm the tortillas in the remaining oil to make them pliable, then dip each into the warm pumpkin-seed sauce. Spoon a bit of chopped egg along the centre, then roll up and place in a casserole or baking dish.

5. Cover with foil and keep warm in a preheated oven at 180°C/350°F/Gas Mark 4 while you heat the tomato and pumpkin-seed sauces, taking care that the pumpkin-seed sauce does not overcook and curdle.

6. Serve the papadzules with pumpkin-seed sauce and tomato sauce spooned over, and pickled onions on the side.

NUTRITIONAL INFORMATION				
	TOTAL FAT	SAT FAT	CHOL	ENERGY
Total	266g	45g	1903mg	4731kcals/19791kJ
Per Serving	44g	7.5g	317mg	788kcals/3298kJ

PAN DE CAZON

LAYERED CASSEROLE OF SHARK AND TORTILLAS, CAMPECHE STYLE

Typical of the Yucatan, these tortillas are usually fried until puffed then slit and stuffed. Here I have simplified the process by layering the tortillas with the stuffing.
Most types of shark are marvellous with the beans, tomato sauce and tortillas; if shark is unavailable, any firm-fleshed fish fillet can be substituted.

SERVES 4

650g/1½lb shark steaks

2½tsp fresh oregano, crumbled

2 onions, chopped

6 cloves garlic, whole but unpeeled

2tbsp orange juice

2tbsp lime juice

grated zest of ½ orange and ¼ lime

1tsp sugar

fish stock cube or 250ml/
8fl oz clam juice mixed with
an equal amount of water
(optional)

salt and pepper

50ml/2fl oz vegetable oil

½ chilli habañero or Scots
bonnet or 2 serrano or
jalapeño chillies, chopped

900g/2lb tomatoes, diced

2tbsp grapefruit juice

1 quantity Frijoles Refritos
(page 12), made with black
beans and seasoned with
chilli, heated through and
kept warm

12 tortillas

TO GARNISH

2–3tbsp chopped fresh
coriander

2 fresh serrano or jalapeño
chillies, thinly sliced

1. Place the shark with 2tsp oregano, half the onion and the whole garlic cloves in a saucepan. Add water to cover, as well as the stock cube or clam juice, if using. Bring to the boil then reduce the heat and simmer very gently for about 10 minutes. Remove from the heat and let the fish cool in the stock. Season with salt and pepper, then remove the fish from the stock and shred or pull apart into small pieces.

2. To make the sauce, heat 30ml/2tbsp oil in a frying pan and fry the remaining onion until softened. Add the chilli, tomatoes and citrus juices and zest. Season with the remaining oregano and thin with a little of the stock from simmering the fish.

3. Warm the tortillas in a small amount of the oil then arrange 4 in a casserole. Spread with warm black beans then top with a layer of fish. Add another tortilla layer and a layer of sauce, then another layer of tortillas, black beans and fish, then a final layer of tortillas and sauce. Cover with foil or a lid and bake for about 10 minutes in a preheated oven at 230°C/450°F/Gas Mark 8. Garnish with fresh coriander and chillies as well as any leftover sauce.

NUTRITIONAL INFORMATION				
	TOTAL FAT	SAT FAT	CHOL	ENERGY
Total	140g	23g	375mg	5574kcals/23556kJ
Per Serving	35g	5.75g	94mg	1394kcals/5889kJ

ENCHILADAS DE ELOTES
CORN ENCHILADAS
WITH TOMATO-RED CHILLI SAUCE

Sweetcorn mixed with cheese, half puréed and half chunky makes a marvellous filling for enchiladas.

SERVES 4

350g/12oz cooked sweetcorn,
lightly drained

100g/4oz cottage or Ricotta
cheese

2 cloves garlic, chopped

about ½ fresh green chilli
such as jalapeño, chopped

salt

pinch of sugar

½tsp ground cumin

2tbsp chopped fresh
coriander

225g/8oz sharp white cheese
such as fresh Pecorino,
Cheddar, or a mixture of
Monterey Jack, Asiago and
Parmesan

9 corn tortillas

1–2tbsp vegetable oil

175g/6oz tomatoes, fresh or
canned, with their juice

85ml/3fl oz vegetable stock

1tbsp mild chilli powder

pinch chipotle chilli powder
(toasted, ground dried
chipotle chilli) or drop
chipotle marinade or salsa

1. Combine the corn with the cottage or Ricotta cheese, half the garlic, the fresh chilli, salt, sugar, cumin, coriander, half the cheese and 1 tortilla, thinly sliced or chopped.

2. Whirl half this mixture in a blender or food processor then combine with with the half that has not been puréed.

3. Heat the remaining tortillas in oil to soften, then spoon a few tablespoons of filling on to the edge of each and roll up. Place each rolled tortilla in a baking dish.

4. Combine the remaining garlic with the tomatoes, vegetable stock, chilli powder, chipotle powder or marinade if using. Spoon over the sauce. Top with the remaining cheese.

5. Bake in a preheated oven at 200°C/400°F/Gas Mark 6 oven until heated through and the cheese topping has melted.

NUTRITIONAL INFORMATION				
	TOTAL FAT	SAT FAT	CHOL	ENERGY
Total	111g	59g	266mg	2922kcals/12297kJ
Per Serving	28g	15g	67mg	730 kcals/3074kJ

ENCHILADAS VERDES

GREEN-TOMATO ENCHILADAS

Enchiladas verdes are one of the most irresistible dishes in the Mexican kitchen. Simple to prepare, the tangy tomatillo sauce balances the richness of the cheese and the heartiness of the tortillas.

Simmered chicken, pork or beef can be used as filling instead of the cheese; in New Mexico these would come with a golden-yolked egg plunked enticingly on top.

SERVES 4

450g/1lb cooked tomatillos, puréed (or use canned)

2 cloves garlic, chopped

1 onion, chopped

½ jalapeño chilli, chopped

1tbsp chopped fresh coriander

120ml/4fl oz chicken or vegetable stock

salt and pepper

⅛tsp ground cumin

10–12 corn tortillas

vegetable oil

450g/1lb mild cheese such as Monterey Jack, Gouda, Mozzarella or Cheddar, or a combination, coarsely grated

soured cream, to garnish

½ onion, chopped, to garnish

fresh salsa of choice, to serve

1. Combine the tomatillos, garlic, onion, jalapeño and coriander with the stock in a pan and bring to the boil. Simmer for 15–25 minutes or just long enough to blend the flavours. Season with salt, pepper and cumin.

2. Warm the tortillas in a lightly oiled heavy-based frying pan then dip into the warm tomatillo sauce. Place 1–2tbsp of grated cheese along one side and roll up, reserving enough cheese for sprinkling on top of the casserole.

3. Arrange in a baking dish. Sprinkle with cheese and cumin, then bake in a preheated oven at 190°C/375°F/Gas Mark 5 until the cheese melts.

4. Serve immediately, garnished with soured cream and chopped onion. Offer salsa of choice on the side.

NUTRITIONAL INFORMATION

	TOTAL FAT	SAT FAT	CHOL	ENERGY
Total	171g	103g	530mg	3406kcals/14272kJ
Per Serving	42g	26g	133mg	851kcals/3568kJ

VARIATION
PASILLA-PAINTED ENCHILADAS VERDES

Lightly toast 2 pasilla chillies, then pour hot water over them. Leave to soak until they rehydrate; to hurry the process simmer for about 20 minutes. When cool enough to handle, remove the stems, open the chillies up and, using a sharp paring knife, remove the seeds and inner veins. Carefully scrape the flesh from the papery skin. Take this rich concentrated pasilla flesh and purée it with 30ml/2fl oz chicken or vegetable stock. Drizzle on to the enchiladas before you sprinkle with cheese, then bake.

ENCHILADAS DE MOLE ROJO

ENCHILADAS IN RED MOLE

This casserole of tortillas dipped in a rich chilli, nut and seed sauce and topped with chickpeas and cheese is a delicious mix of complex earthy flavours.

This is an elaboration of a similar enchilada I ate on a bus ride through the mountains of Mexico's interior. At various points in the seemingly endless and sometimes perilous drive our bus stopped in little villages for rest and food. Women came out bearing earthenware casseroles filled with a wide variety of dishes prepared for us, all for but a few pesos.

SERVES 4

- 2tbsp toasted sesame seeds
- 2–3tbsp roasted peanuts
- 2tbsp ancho chilli powder
- 1tbsp hot paprika or very mild chilli powder (or soak 3 ancho chillies then purée with a little of the soaking liquid)
- ⅛–¼tsp ground cinnamon
- pinch of ground cloves
- ⅛–¼tsp dried thyme
- ⅛–¼tsp dried oregano
- ⅛–¼tsp dried marjoram
- pinch of pepper
- 350ml/12fl oz water
- salt
- 3 cloves garlic, crushed
- 45–60ml/3–4tbsp oil
- juice of 1 lime
- 12 corn tortillas
- approx 12oz cooked beef
- 350g/12oz cooked, drained chickpeas

a little chicken or vegetable stock

100g/4oz fresh white cheese such as Gueso Fresco, fresh Pecorino or a not too salty Feta, lightly crumbled

TO SERVE

1 waxy potato, boiled and cubed

1 carrot, boiled and cubed

5ml/1tsp vinegar

shredded lettuce

225g/8oz soured cream

2tbsp chopped fresh coriander

2 spring onions, thinly sliced

jalapeños en escabeche

1. In a spice or coffee grinder, grind the sesame seeds and peanuts to a fine meal.

2. Place it with the chilli powder and paprika (or puréed chillies), cinnamon, cloves, thyme, oregano, marjoram, pepper, water, salt and garlic in a blender or food processor and whirl to make a smooth sauce.

3. Heat 15–30ml/2–3tbsp oil in a frying pan then pour in the sauce. Cook, scraping up the bottom, for about 10 minutes or until the sauce becomes rich in flavour and darkened in colour. Stir in the lime juice and set aside.

4. Heat the tortillas in an oiled pan until softened, then spread each with some of the red chilli and seed sauce. Fill with a few spoonfuls of meat then roll up. Arrange each rolled tortilla in a casserole. When all the tortillas have been filled, sprinkle with chickpeas and the remaining sauce.

5. Spoon over a little chicken or vegetable stock then sprinkle with cheese. Place in a preheated oven at 200°C/400°F/Gas Mark 6 and heat through until the enchiladas are hot and the cheese is melted.

6. Toss the potato and carrot with vinegar.

7. Serve garnished with potato and carrot, lettuce, soured cream, coriander, spring onions and jalapeños en escabeche.

NUTRITIONAL INFORMATION

	TOTAL FAT	SAT FAT	CHOL	ENERGY
Total	151g	58g	238mg	3525kcals/14804kJ
Per Serving	38g	14g	59mg	881kcals/3701kJ

LOWER FAT VARIATION

Substitute fromage frais for soured cream and use a low-fat cheese.

SOPA SECA DE FIDEOS

DRY SOUP OF PASTA

IN MILD CHILLI SAUCE WITH CHEESE

Sopa seca translates literally as "dry soup", a name given to pasta and rice dishes cooked in broth to a thick, casserole-like consistency. It is a consummate comfort food, as good eaten with a spoon alone late at night as it is in a more sociable setting, sitting around the table.

SERVES 4

350g/12oz very thin pasta such as capellini, nidi, or coiled fideo

2–3 bay leaves

2–3 Mexican chorizo sausages, about 75g/3oz each, cut into bite-sized pieces (or spicy, unsmoked Spanish chorizo)

1 onion, chopped

1 green pepper or mild green chilli such as Anaheim or poblano, thinly sliced

4–5 cloves garlic, chopped

350ml/12fl oz tomato sauce, chopped tomatoes or passata

350ml/12fl oz hot but not boiling chicken, meat or vegetable stock

crumbled dry oregano to taste

350g/12oz sharp cheese or combination creamy mild cheese and sharp cheese, coarsely grated

2tbsp chopped fresh coriander

1. Boil the pasta with the bay leaves until the pasta is just al dente. Drain and discard bay leaves.

2. Fry the chorizo; when it begins to brown add the onion and pepper or chilli and continue to cook until they have softened. Add the garlic, tomato sauce, chopped tomatoes or passata, stock and oregano.

3. Toss the drained pasta with the sauce mixture then place in a baking dish. Cover with grated cheese.

4. Bake in a preheated oven at 200°C/400°F/Gas Mark 6 until the top is bubbling and lightly browned and the dish is heated well through. Serve immediately, with fresh coriander.

NUTRITIONAL INFORMATION

	TOTAL FAT	SAT FAT	CHOL	ENERGY
Total	194g	106g	482mg	3800kcals/15832kJ
Per Serving	48.5g	26.5g	121mg	950kcals/3958kJ

PAELLA

Sunday lunch in the Colonial regions and restaurants of Mexico is time for paella. And what a paella you will find! Rich with a sea-full of creatures, spicy and redolent of garlic, scented with chorizo. Unlike paella in Spain and the Languedoc, paella in Mexico is at its best when accompanied by a bowl of fresh spicy salsa.

Your lunch might begin with a crisp spicy ceviche of whatever is freshest from the sea: tangy with lemon and cooked by the citrus juice, not heat. Warm tortillas accompany the paella, with crisp cooling beer to drink, and afterwards perhaps a dessert of lush tropical fruits or a bowl of comforting eggy crème caramel, perhaps scented with coffee.

SERVES 6 - 8

1tsp dried oregano	200ml/7fl oz tomato passata or 225g/8oz fresh or canned tomatoes, chopped
5 cloves garlic, chopped	
5ml/1tsp vinegar	1 l/1¾pt hot chicken stock
30ml/2tbsp olive oil	2 large pinches saffron, lightly toasted in an ungreased pan, then crushed in mortar and pestle
1tsp salt	
1 chicken or rabbit, cut into serving pieces	
2 chorizos, skinned and chopped	225g/8oz squid, cleaned and cut into rings and tentacles
1 onion, chopped	175g/6oz prawns in their shells
1 red pepper, diced	225g/8oz peas, blanched or young green beans, topped and tailed and cut into bite-sized lengths
1 green pepper, diced	
1tsp ground coriander	
450g/1lb long-grain easy-cook rice	175g/6oz marinated artichoke hearts (optional)
	450g/1lb clams or mussels

1. Toss the oregano, garlic, vinegar, olive oil and salt with the chicken or rabbit. Leave to marinate for at least 30 minutes, preferably overnight.

2. Remove from the marinade. Save any marinade to add when cooking the rice.

3. Fry the chicken with the chorizo in a heavy-based frying pan until the chicken is lightly browned and cooked about halfway through and the chorizo has broken into bits. Do not let the chorizo burn; remove it from the pan if it cooks before the chicken.

4. Remove the chicken and chorizo from the pan, leaving behind the savoury flavoured oil from the cooking. In this cook the onion and peppers, letting them fry lightly until softened. Stir in the coriander and cook for a few moments longer.

5. Stir in the rice and cook lightly in the onion-pepper mixture then add the tomatoes and stir in the hot stock. Return the chicken, the chorizo, and any juices that have accumulated, as well as any marinade left over to the pan with the rice and stock. Add the saffron. Cover and cook for about 10 minutes or until the rice is half cooked.

6. Fold in the squid, prawns, peas or beans and marinated artichoke hearts, if using, then top the casserole with the clams or mussels. Cover and bake in a preheated oven at 230°C/450°F/Gas Mark 8 for about 10 minutes longer or until the clams or mussels pop open. Serve immediately.

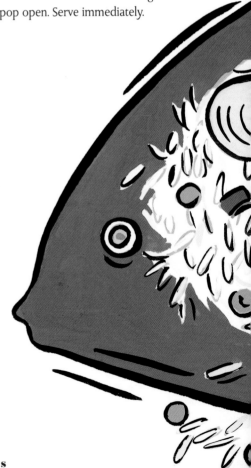

NUTRITIONAL INFORMATION				
	TOTAL FAT	SAT FAT	CHOL	ENERGY
Total	126g	37g	1600mg	4672kcals/19721kJ
Serving (6)	21g	6g	267mg	779kcals/3287kJ
Serving (8)	16g	4.5g	200mg	584kcals/2465kJ

HUEVOS

EGG DISHES

Mexican cuisine is rich in egg dishes – in fact, my favourite dish, although too simple to require a recipe, is a mound of steamed rice topped with 2 poached eggs, lots of sparklingly fresh tomato-green chilli salsa and a sprinkling of coriander.

HUEVOS CON TOTOPOS (MIGAS)

EGGS SCRAMBLED

WITH TOMATOES, CHILLIES AND TORTILLAS

Scrambled with tomatoes, chillies, garlic and spices, with a handful of crisp tortilla chips stirred in, eggs make a marvellous supper or brunch dish.

SERVES 4

8–10 corn tortillas, cut into 12mm/½in strips (or several large handfuls not too salty or oily tortilla chips)

100ml/4fl oz vegetable oil

6 cloves garlic, chopped

1 green pepper, diced

½ jalapeño or other green chilli, thinly sliced or chopped

40g/1½oz butter

1½tsp ground cumin

5 ripe tomatoes, coarsely chopped

8 eggs, lightly beaten

TO GARNISH

3tbsp chopped fresh coriander

3–4 spring onions, thinly sliced

1. Fry the tortilla strips in the oil until golden but not dark brown; remove from the oil and drain on paper towels. (If using tortilla chips simply break up into bite-sized pieces.)

2. Fry the garlic, green pepper and chilli in a third of the butter for just 1 minute, then add the cumin and tomatoes and cook over medium heat for 3–4 minutes until the tomatoes are no longer runny. Remove from the pan and set aside.

3. Over low heat, melt the remaining butter in a pan. Pour in the beaten eggs. Cook over low heat, stirring until the eggs begin to set.

4. Add the reserved chilli-tomato mixture and tortilla strips and continue cooking, stirring once or twice, until the eggs are the consistency you wish. The tortilla strips should be pliable and chewy, neither crisp nor soggy.

5. Serve immediately, topped with coriander and spring onions.

NUTRITIONAL INFORMATION				
	TOTAL FAT	SAT FAT	CHOL	ENERGY
Total	222g	55g	2007mg	3590kcals/15005kJ
Per Serving	55.5g	13.5g	502mg	897kcals/3751kJ

LOWER FAT VARIATION

Prepare the tortillas as for Fat-Free Totopos (page 11) and omit the oil for frying.

HUEVOS A LA MEXICANA
MEXICAN EGGS

This simple dish consists of egg-topped tortillas, covered with a layer of tangy cheese, studded with chillies and tomatoes and seasoned with garlic. Serve with tender beans, either pinto or black, and rice tinted golden with saffron. Serve your favourite fresh salsa on the side, along with a salad of avocado, roasted red pepper, sliced orange and red onion.

SERVES 4

drizzle of butter or olive oil

4 corn tortillas

2 cloves garlic, chopped

1–2 green chillies, chopped

3–4 ripe tomatoes, diced

4 eggs, broken into saucers, yolks whole and intact

½tsp ground cumin or cumin seeds

175g/6oz grated or crumbled cheese such as Pecorino or a mixture of Monterey Jack and Feta

TO GARNISH

2tbsp chopped onion

2tbsp chopped fresh coriander

1. Use a pan that is big enough to take all the tortillas or use two pans. Heat a small amount of butter or oil in the pan(s) and add the tortillas. Scatter the tops of the tortillas with the garlic, green chilli and tomatoes then carefully pour an egg on to each tortilla. Sprinkle with cumin and cheese, cover, and cook over medium low heat until the whites of the egg have firmed and the cheese melted, though the yolks should remain soft.

2. Scatter with onion and coriander and serve immediately.

NUTRITIONAL INFORMATION				
	TOTAL FAT	SAT FAT	CHOL	ENERGY
Total	65g	31g	1074mg	1401kcals/5883kJ
Per Serving	16g	8g	269mg	350kcals/1471kJ

HUEVOS MOTULENOS
TOMATO-CHILLI EGGS

In the Yucatan this classic dish would come sandwiched between two crisp tortillas, but I find that with tortillas on the bottom only, the dish is more visually appealing.

SERVES 4

400g/14oz fresh or canned tomatoes, chopped

1 onion, chopped

3 cloves garlic, crushed

1–2 fresh chillies, chopped

salt and pepper

large pinch of ground cumin

45ml/3tbsp olive oil

1 plantain, peeled and diced

15g/½oz butter

4 tostadas (page 11)

Frijoles Refritos (page 12), seasoned with cumin

4 or 8 poached or fried eggs, warm

1 red pepper or fresh large red mild chilli such as Anaheim or poblano, roasted, seeded, stemmed and peeled, then cut into strips

3–4tbsp cooked green peas, warm

3tbsp diced ham

2tbsp chopped fresh coriander

50–75g/2–3oz flavourful white cheese such as Feta or mild white such as Monterey Jack, diced

1. In a blender or food processor, purée tomatoes with the onion, garlic, chillies, salt and pepper and cumin.

2. Heat the oil in a frying pan then ladle in a little of this sauce and cook until the sauce reduces in volume and becomes almost paste-like. Ladle in some more sauce and repeat. Finally, pour in the remaining sauce and simmer together for 5–10 minutes. Keep warm.

3. Lightly brown the plantain in butter. Set aside and keep warm.

4. Spread the tostadas with warm Frijoles Negros Refritos, then top each with 1 or 2 poached or fried egg(s).

5. Spoon the warm tomato sauce around and/or over the egg, then sprinkle with the diced plantains, roasted peppers or chillies, peas, ham, coriander and cheese.

NUTRITIONAL INFORMATION				
	TOTAL FAT	SAT FAT	CHOL	ENERGY
Total	157g	45.5g	1045mg	4494kcals/18932kJ
Per Serving	39g	11.3g	261mg	1123kcals/4733kJ

HUEVOS OAXAQUENA
OAXACA EGGS

Cooking eggs in a flat omelette, then cutting them into strips makes an intriguingly different egg dish .

SERVES 4

900g/2lb tomatoes

pinch of sugar

6 small to medium-sized onions, peeled and halved

10 cloves garlic, whole and unpeeled

2–3 Anaheim or poblano chillies, roasted, peeled and sliced

3 fresh green chillies such as serranos, thinly sliced

75ml/3fl oz oil

salt and pepper

pinch of cumin

pinch of dried oregano

pinch of sugar

8 eggs, lightly beaten

TO GARNISH

2tbsp chopped fresh coriander

a little chopped fresh chilli (optional)

1. In an ungreased heavy-based pan, lightly char the tomatoes, turning once or twice. Allow to cool.

2. Cut up the tomatoes and place in a blender or food processor with their skins. Lightly char the onions and garlic. Cut up the onions and add to the blender or food processor, then squeeze the garlic cloves out of their skins and add with the chillies. Whirl until a smooth purée is formed.

3. Heat 30ml/2tbsp oil in a frying pan then ladle in the sauce. Cook over high heat until it thickens and condenses.

4. Season to taste with salt and pepper, cumin, oregano and sugar to balance the acid-sweetness. Set aside.

5. Make flat omelettes, like thin pancakes, in the remaining oil, cooking about 2 eggs at a time and turning them over. Stack on a plate, and slice into noodle-like ribbons.

6. Heat the omelette strips in the sauce until warmed through, then garnish with coriander and a little fresh chilli.

NUTRITIONAL INFORMATION				
	TOTAL FAT	SAT FAT	CHOL	ENERGY
Total	145g	25g	1903mg	1811kcals/7525kJ
Per Serving	36g	6.25g	476mg	453kcals/1881kJ

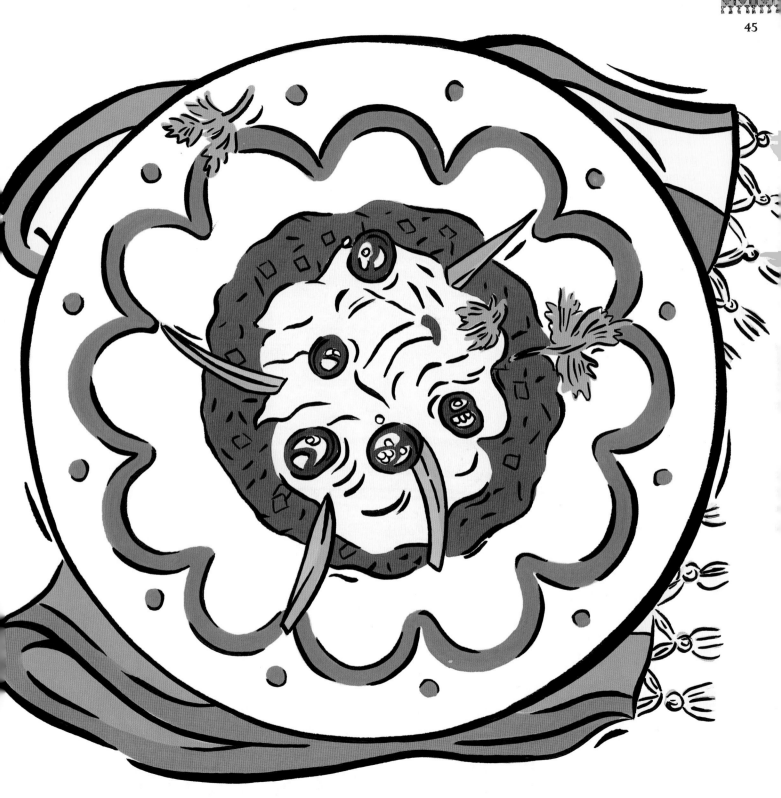

CASSEROLES, EGG DISHES AND VEGETARIAN MEALS

PATATAS CON CHIPOTLE CREMA Y QUESO DE CABRITA

POTATOES

WITH GOAT'S CHEESE-CHIPOTLE
CREAM

This makes a luscious casserole of potatoes baked with tangy goat's cheese and piquant chipotle, rich with cream and melted cheese. Serve with a crisp salad of purslane, chervil, watercress, and other interesting greens, lightly dressed with olive oil and vinegar.

SERVES 4

1.5kg/3lb baking potatoes, peeled and cut into chunks

salt and pepper

200g/7oz crème fraîche

120ml/4fl oz vegetarian stock

4 cloves garlic, chopped

1–2tsp marinade from chipotles en adobo, or ½ chopped chipotle or mild chilli powder to taste

1 log (225g/8oz) goat's cheese, sliced

175g/6oz melting white cheese such as Queso Anejo, medium Asiago, Monterey Jack, Mozzarella, grated

50–75g/2–3oz Parmesan or Pecorino, grated

1. Cook the potatoes in rapidly boiling water until half done. Drain and sprinkle with salt and pepper.

2. Combine the crème fraîche with the stock, half the garlic, and the chipotle marinade, chipotle or chilli powder.

3. Arrange half the potatoes in a baking casserole then pour half the crème fraîche sauce over the potatoes. Add a layer of goat's cheese, then finish with the remaining potatoes and sauce.

4. Sprinkle with grated white cheese then with grated Parmesan or Pecorino.

5. Bake in a preheated oven at 180–190°C/350–375°F/Gas Mark 4–5 until the potatoes are creamy inside and the cheese topping is lightly golden and crisped in places on top. Serve immediately, sprinkled with the remaining garlic.

NUTRITIONAL INFORMATION				
	TOTAL FAT	SAT FAT	CHOL	ENERGY
Total	140g	86g	294mg	3194kcals/13392kJ
Per Serving	35g	21.5g	73mg	798kcals/3348kJ

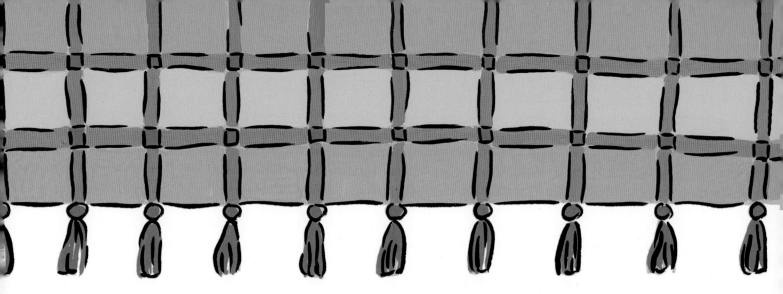

CHAPTER FOUR

BARBECUED
AND GRILLED FOODS

★ ★ ★ ★ ★

BARBECUED AND GRILLED FOODS

The scent of smoke permeates the air throughout Mexico. In the markets, braziers are set up for impromptu tacos al carbon. In the countryside, a fiesta means a great pit will be dug for a barbacoa, and in restaurants wood-fired grills flavour a wide variety of foods from the land and sea.

CARNE ASADO CON PLATANOS Y SALSA

GRILLED RARE STEAK AND PLANTAINS

WITH CHIPOTLE-TOMATO SALSA

The roasty, meaty flavour of rare steak cooked over the coals is enhanced by a dab of smoky chipotle salsa. Ripe plantains, browned over the coals as well, provide a sweet, starchy sidenote. A bed of greens is refreshing next to the rich meat and plantains; purslane especially is *muy Mexicana*, though usually simmered in a stew rather than served raw. Purslane is seldom sold in grocery shops; the best place to find it is between the plants in your garden. It is a creeping, flat-lying plant that has slightly rounded, almost succulent little leaves. It is unusual and delicious, and recent reports suggest it may be a good source of omega-3 fatty acids. Serve with a mound of rice and black beans, and a bowl of the fiery salsa.

SERVES 4

4 tender steaks such as fillet, about 175g/6oz each

3 cloves garlic, chopped

salt and pepper

15ml/1tbsp olive oil

2 ripe plantains, peeled and cut into halves lengthwise

pinch of ground cinnamon

few drops of chipotle marinade or ¼–½ chipotle chilli en adobo, chopped

400g/14oz fresh or canned tomatoes, chopped

½ onion, chopped

pinch of ground cumin

pinch of dried oregano

TO GARNISH

wedges of lime

handful of greens such as watercress, purslane, rocket, or coriander

1. Rub the meat with about 1 clove of chopped garlic, then sprinkle with salt and pepper. Rub with olive oil and set aside.

2. Sprinkle the plantains with cinnamon and set aside.

3. To make the salsa, combine the chipotle marinade or chopped chipotle with the tomatoes, onion and remaining garlic; season with cinnamon, cumin, the oregano and salt and pepper.

4. Cook the steaks over hot coals until lightly charred on the outside, rare within. Depending on the thickness, they should take only about 3–4 minutes on each side.

5. Add the plantains to the grill and cook until lightly browned in spots, about 3 minutes on each side.

6. Serve the steak and plantains garnished with lime wedges, a handful of greens and chipotle salsa.

NUTRITIONAL INFORMATION				
	TOTAL FAT	SAT FAT	CHOL	ENERGY
Total	45g	15g	413mg	1512 kcals/6384kJ
Per Serving	11g	4g	103mg	378kcals/1596kJ

YUCATECAN STEAK

Barbecuing a handful of spring onions alongside whatever else is on the grill is *muy Mexicana*. Cut the onions on the diagonal as otherwise the long strands can stick in the throat.

SERVES 4

4 thin steaks, beef, pork or venison

3 cloves garlic, chopped

30ml/2tbsp tequila

2tbsp mild red chilli powder

2tbsp chopped fresh coriander

juice of ½ orange

juice of 2 or more limes

6–10 spring onions, trimmed

90ml/6tbsp olive oil

½ onion, grated

salt

½ white or green cabbage, thinly sliced

pinch of dried oregano

½ green chilli, thinly sliced

TO SERVE

1 recipe batch of black beans (page 12), refried or simmered with chillies

corn tortillas

salsa of choice

wedges of lime and orange

1. Combine the steaks with the garlic, tequila, chilli powder, coriander, orange juice, 15ml/1tbsp lime juice, spring onions, half the olive oil, grated onion and salt to taste. Leave to marinate for about 30 minutes.

2. Combine the cabbage with the oregano, green chilli, remaining olive oil and lime juice, and salt to taste. (This cabbage relish is even better prepared a day ahead.)

3. Grill the steaks and spring onions over hot coals quickly until they are just cooked. Since they are thin, they need only cook a few minutes on each side.

4. Slice the spring onions into more easily chewable slices and serve alongside the steaks. Accompany with black beans, corn tortillas, salsa, and wedges of lime and orange.

NUTRITIONAL INFORMATION				
	TOTAL FAT	SAT FAT	CHOL	ENERGY
Total	87g	17.5g	236mg	1348kcals/5608kJ
Per Serving	22g	4.5g	59mg	337kcals/1402kJ

POLLO ROJO CON SALSA DE AGUACATE

RED CHILLI-MARINATED CHICKEN BREASTS
WITH AVOCADO SAUCE

Sauces of mashed avocado are frequently spooned up with grilled foods. Their bland flavour balances the spicy scent of the barbecue and the piquant jolt of chilli.

SERVES 4

4 boneless chicken breasts, 200–225g/7–8oz each, skin removed	30ml/2tbsp olive oil
	juice of 1 lime
45ml/3tbsp Recado Rojo (page 19) (or mix a good chilli powder with chopped garlic, orange juice and zest, plus a pinch of ground cumin)	2tbsp chopped fresh coriander
	2 ripe avocados, peeled and lightly mashed
	¼ onion, chopped

1. Combine the chicken breasts with 35ml/2tbsp Recado Rojo, the olive oil, half the lime juice and half the coriander. Leave to marinate for at least 30 minutes.

2. To make the sauce, combine the remaining lime juice and coriander with the avocados and remaining Recado Rojo. Season with salt to taste and set aside, covered.

3. Grill the chicken breasts, about 3 minutes per side. Do not overcook.

4. Serve the chicken breasts hot from the barbecue, sprinkled with onion and napped with the spicy avocado sauce.

NUTRITIONAL INFORMATION

	TOTAL FAT	SAT FAT	CHOL	ENERGY
Total	85g	19g	344mg	1520kcals/6355kJ
Per Serving	21g	4.75g	86mg	380kcals/1589kJ

VARIATION
GRILLED STEAK WITH SALSA DE AGUACATE

In place of chicken breasts, grill tender steaks, rubbed with the same spicy mixture. Cook until rare, only a few minutes on each side.

POLLO ROJO A LA PARILLA

BARBECUED CHICKEN
MARINATED IN ACHIOTE
AND MUSTARD

Achiote seeds, ground into a bright orange powder, have a slightly tangy, slightly saffron scent. They colour everything they touch an indelible yellow hue. This is a delicious grilled chicken dish that I tasted in Mexico City.

SERVES 4

1 chicken, 900g–1.5kg/2–3lb, halved or quartered	75ml/5tbsp mild brown flavourful mustard, preferably wholeseed
2tbsp achiote seeds, ground or puréed	45ml/3tbsp Dijon mustard
8 cloves garlic, thinly sliced	45ml/3tbsp olive oil
1 onion, finely chopped, or 5–8 shallots, chopped	30ml/2tbsp lemon juice
1tbsp sweet paprika	45ml/3tbsp crème fraîche or soured cream
2tbsp mild chilli powder	salt and pepper

1. Combine the chicken with the ground or puréed garlic, onion or shallots, paprika, chilli powder, half the mild mustard, the Dijon mustard, olive oil and lemon juice.

2. Leave to marinate in the refrigerator, at least overnight and up to 2 days.

3. Cook over medium-hot coals, putting the leg quarters on the grill for 15 minutes (chicken halves take longer, around 20 minutes), then adding the breast quarters and cooking for a further 15 minutes. The chicken is done when the juices run clear when the flesh is pierced.

4. Meanwhile, combine the reserved mustard with the crème fraîche or soured cream.

5. Spread the mustard-crème fraîche mixture over the hot chicken, then sprinkle with salt and pepper. Serve immediately.

NUTRITIONAL INFORMATION

	TOTAL FAT	SAT FAT	CHOL	ENERGY
Total	90g	24g	657mg	1697kcals/7103kJ
Per Serving	22.5g	6g	164mg	424kcals/1776kJ

PESCADO A LA PARILLA

BACON-WRAPPED TROUT
WITH RED CHILLI ESSENCE

This is a modern adaptation of the escabeche, that is, lightly pickled, sauce: here, reduced stock is seasoned with vinegar, then poured over a hot grilled fish.

SERVES 4

1 onion, chopped

3 cloves garlic, chopped

2tbsp olive oil

2 ripe tomatoes, chopped

1–3tbsp mild chilli powder

¼tsp ground cumin

350ml/12fl oz chicken stock

175ml/6fl oz dry white wine

30ml/2tbsp vinegar

4 small to medium-sized trout, cleaned (leave head or remove, as desired)

salt and pepper

4–8 slices smoked bacon, derinded

fresh coriander leaves, to garnish

1. Fry the onion and garlic in olive oil until softened; do not allow to brown. Add the tomatoes, then stir in the chilli powder and cumin and cook for a few moments.

2. Pour in the stock and wine; boil until it reduces in volume to about 175ml/6fl oz then add the vinegar. Simmer for another 5 minutes, or until it tastes tangy and flavourful, then remove from the heat.

3. Sprinkle each trout with salt and pepper then wrap with bacon, using 1 or 2 rashers per trout, as needed.

4. Grill over hot coals, about 5 minutes per side, or until the fish feels done when gently pressed with the finger.

5. Serve each portion of trout in a bowl with a few spoonfuls of the chilli essence poured over. Garnish with coriander.

NUTRITIONAL INFORMATION				
	TOTAL FAT	SAT FAT	CHOL	ENERGY
Total	61g	12g	426mg	1306kcals/5475kJ
Per Serving	15g	3g	107mg	326kcals/1369kJ

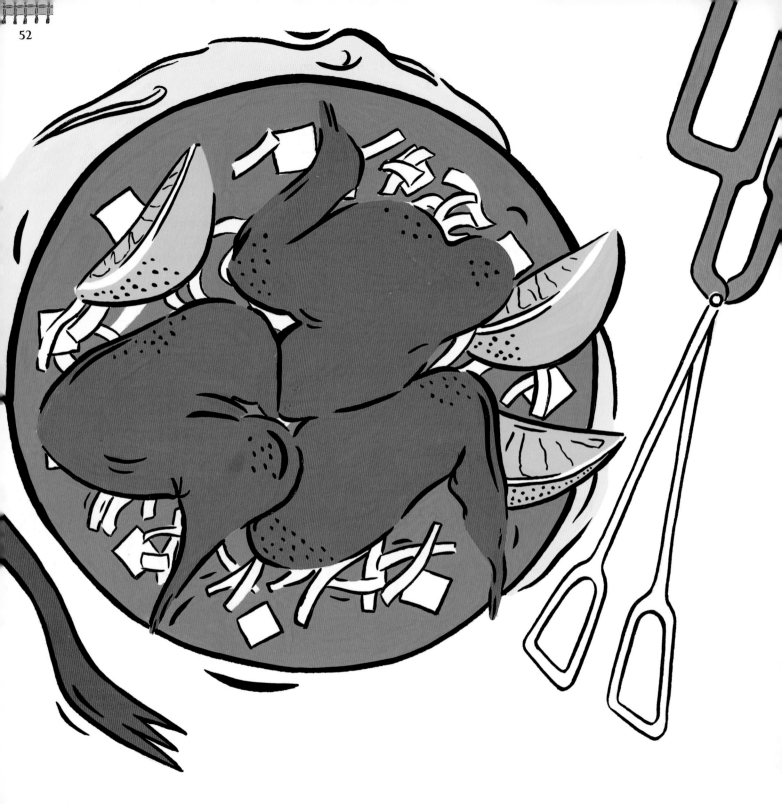

POLLO CON CHILE Y TEQUILA

CHILLI-TEQUILA-MARINATED CRISP CHICKEN WINGS

Chilli spices season the chicken wings while tequila and citrus juice tenderize them. These are delicious served on their own or with other barbecued foods such as seafood, sausages and so forth, all accompanied by steamed rice and black beans, and plantains cooked on the grill.

SERVES 4

900g–1.5kg/2–3lb chicken wings

5 cloves garlic, chopped

juice of 2 limes

juice of 1 orange

30ml/2tbsp tequila

salt and pepper

1tbsp mild chilli powder

10ml/2tsp chipotle marinade or 3 dried chipotle chillies, rehydrated and puréed

30ml/2tbsp vegetable oil

1tsp sugar

¼tsp ground allspice

pinch of ground cinnamon

pinch of ground cumin

pinch of dried oregano, crumbled

1. Combine the chicken wings with all the other ingredients and leave to marinate for at least 3 hours, preferably overnight.

2. Cook over hot coals for approximately 15–25 minutes, until the wings are crisply browned, and serve immediately.

NUTRITIONAL INFORMATION				
	TOTAL FAT	SAT FAT	CHOL	ENERGY
Total	56g	13g	475mg	1260 kcals/5277kJ
Per Serving	14g	3g	119mg	315kcals/1319kJ

POLLITO CON SALSA CREMA, PIMIENTO ROJO, Y CHILLI CHIPOTLE

GREEN-HERBED POUSSIN
WITH ROASTED RED PEPPER-CHIPOTLE CREAM

This tender poussin dish is both elegant and rustic, and is marvellously accompanied by Mexican rice cooked with kernels of sweet corn and a sprinkling of fresh marjoram.

SERVES 4

10 cloves garlic, chopped

juice of 1 lime

45ml/3tbsp olive oil

50g/2oz chopped coriander, plus a little extra for garnish

½ green chilli, chopped

1tsp ground cumin

4 poussins, spatchcocked

salt and pepper

350g/12oz crème fraîche or soured cream

1 red pepper, roasted, peeled, and diced

½–1tsp marinade from chipotles en adobo

3–5 spring onions, thinly sliced, to garnish (optional)

1. In a blender or food processor, combine 9 cloves garlic with the lime juice, olive oil, coriander, green chilli and half the cumin. Whirl until it forms a paste.

2. Sprinkle the poussins with salt and pepper, then rub well with the green spicy paste. Leave to marinate for at least 30 minutes at room temperature or up to 48 hours in the refrigerator.

3. Combine the remaining garlic and cumin with the crème fraîche, roasted red pepper and chipotle marinade.

4. Grill the poussin over hot coals or roast in oven at 180°C/350°F/Gas Mark 4 for 35–40 minutes, turning once or twice, until the birds are golden and crisp on the outside, juicy within, about 20 minutes in total on the barbecue.

5. Serve the poussin garnished with the red pepper-chipotle cream and a sprinkling of coriander and/or spring onion.

NUTRITIONAL INFORMATION				
	TOTAL FAT	SAT FAT	CHOL	ENERGY
Total	154g	65g	855mg	2396kcals/9986kJ
Per Serving	38.5g	16g	214mg	599kcals/2497kJ

PESCADO CHIPOTLE CON SALSA DE
CALABACITAS Y CREMA ACIDA

CHIPOTLE-GRILLED SALMON

WITH THREE-SQUASH SALSA AND SOURED CREAM

SERVES 4

4 salmon steaks or fillets,
each 175–225g/6–8oz

30ml/2tbsp olive oil

pinch of ground allspice

pinch of ground cinnamon

juice of 1 lime

5–10ml/1–2tsp chipotle
marinade or chipotle en
adobo sauce or 1 dried
chipotle, rehydrated and
puréed (page 8)

4 cloves garlic, chopped

¼tsp cumin

salt and black pepper

1 courgette, finely diced

175g/6oz yellow squash,
finely diced

175g/6oz pale green squash,
such as patty pan, finely
diced

½ onion, finely chopped

1–2 tomatoes, diced

¼tsp ground cumin

2tsp chopped fresh marjoram
or oregano

soured cream, to serve

1. Combine the salmon with half the olive oil, the allspice, cinnamon, half the lime juice, the chipotle marinade or adobo, half the garlic, cumin, salt and pepper. Leave to marinate for 30–60 minutes.

2. Meanwhile, make the salsa: cook the courgette and squash in boiling water or a steamer until just al dente. Drain and toss with the remaining oil and lime juice, the remaining garlic, the onion, tomatoes, cumin, and marjoram or fresh oregano. Set aside.

3. Grill the salmon over hot coals until just cooked through, 3–4 minutes each side, then serve each portion with 1–2tbsp salsa and a dab of soured cream.

NUTRITIONAL INFORMATION			
	TOTAL FAT	SAT FAT	CHOL	ENERGY
Total	100g	16.5g	350mg	1581kcals/6585kJ
Per Serving	25g	4g	88mg	395kcals/1646kJ

CAMARONES TROPICALES A LA PARILLA

RED CHILLI-SEASONED PRAWNS

WITH TROPICAL FRUIT

Keeping the shells on the prawns during their cooking keeps the little creatures succulent and juicy, though they are a bit messy to eat. Provide a little dish for the shells and warm cloths to wash chilli-stained fingertips.

SERVES 4

675g/1½lb prawns in their
shells

1tbsp achiote seeds, ground
or puréed (page 19)

3tbsp mild chilli powder

1tbsp sweet paprika

5 cloves garlic, chopped

1tsp salt

30ml/2tbsp olive oil

juice of 1 orange

juice of 1 lime

pinch of dried oregano

¼tsp ground cumin

TO GARNISH

handful of bitter salad greens
such as endive

1 ripe mango, peeled and
diced or sliced

1 ripe papaya, peeled and
seeded, cut into the same
size as the mango

1 lime, cut into wedges

handful of fresh coriander
leaves or fresh mint leaves or
both

1. Combine the prawns with the achiote, chilli powder, paprika, garlic, salt, olive oil, orange and lime juice, oregano and cumin. Leave to marinate for at least 30 minutes.

2. Thread on to skewers and grill over hot coals just long enough to cook through but not overcook, about 2–3 minutes per side.

3. Serve on a platter garnished with endive, mango, papaya, lime wedges and coriander and/or mint leaves.

NUTRITIONAL INFORMATION			
	TOTAL FAT	SAT FAT	CHOL	ENERGY
Total	25g	4g	788mg	627kcals/2649kJ
Per Serving	6g	1g	197mg	157kcals/662kJ

LANGOSTA A LA PARILLA

LOBSTER COOKED ON THE GRILL AS IN ROSARITA BEACH

Cooking lobsters on the coals gives them a lovely smoky scent that is enhanced by the spicy red chilli. Serve with creamy frijoles refritos, soft warm corn tortillas, wedges of lime, and a salsa of choice.

Rosarita Beach near Ensenada in Mexico's Baja California is known for its lobster. In the heyday of Hollywood, before the jet made travel so accessible, Ensenada was a weekend getaway for film stars and directors. The exquisitely fresh lobsters that were hauled from the depths of the sea were also part of the allure: grilled over hot coals, then eaten with warm beans, corn tortillas and chilli salsa.

The spicy butter-basted lobster can be baked instead of barbecued: slather it with the butter and place in a hot oven until it sizzles and is warmed through.

SERVES 4

100g/4oz butter, softened	salt and pepper
4 cloves garlic, chopped	2 lobsters, cut through the middle into two halves, or 4 lobster tails, the meat loosened slightly from its shell
2–4tsp mild chilli powder	
3–5tbsp chopped fresh coriander	
juice of ½ lime or lemon	

1. Mix the butter with the garlic, chilli powder, coriander, lime or lemon juice and salt and pepper.

2. Spread on to the cut side of the lobster or lobster tails, getting the spicy butter into all the cracks.

3. Cook on the hot coals, cut side up, preferably covered, so that the top is able to brown lightly. Barbecue for about 15 minutes or until heated through, lightly browned and sizzling. Serve immediately.

NUTRITIONAL INFORMATION				
	TOTAL FAT	SAT FAT	CHOL	ENERGY
Total	108g	69g	688mg	1304kcals/5414kJ
Per Serving	27g	17g	172mg	326kcals/1354kJ

MELLEJONES

BARBECUED MUSSELS IN THEIR SHELLS

Many recipes direct scrubbing mussels to rid them of their beard, but I find that cooking mussels on the barbecue makes this step unnecessary. Soaking in salt water seems to be advantageous, however, as the salt water is similar to the sea and I – perhaps irrationally – think it relaxes the little creatures and results in a more tender dish.

SERVES 4

2 quarts mussels in their shells	Salsa de Limon y Cilantro (page 19)
salt	

1. Place the mussels in a shallow bowl or pan and fill with water to cover. Sprinkle in a generous amount of salt and leave for up to 30 minutes.

2. Place the mussels on a medium low barbecue, and cook, preferably covered, until the mussels pop open, about 10 minutes.

3. Serve the mussels along with the salsa.

NUTRITIONAL INFORMATION				
	TOTAL FAT	SAT FAT	CHOL	ENERGY
Total	15g	2.2g	320mg	808kcals/3438kJ
Per Serving	3.75g	0.5g	80mg	202kcals/859kJ

VARIATION
BARBECUED CLAMS WITH SALSA

Use clams instead of mussels. Salsa de Muchos Chilles y Jitomates (page 18) is good in addition to the coriander salsa.

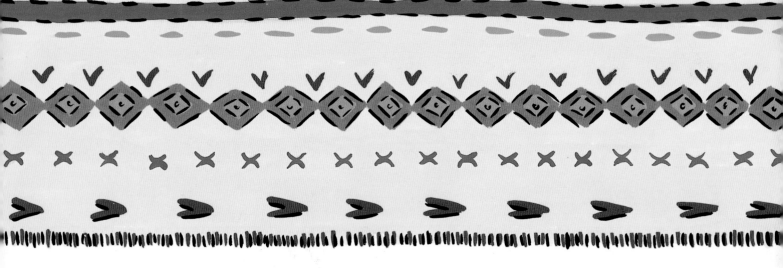

CHAPTER FIVE

BRAISED, STEWED AND ROASTED DISHES

★ ★ ★ ★ ★

SOUPS AND STEWS

The Mexican kitchen is rich with hearty main-course soups: dishes that exude the aroma of comfort, some so thick you can leave a spoon standing up in them. Soup-stews such as posole, birria and menudo are rumoured to cure the eater of all maladies, ranging from a hangover to sexual impairment!

BIRRIA

STEAMED LAMB
SERVED WITH A SAVOURY BROTH

While the original birria is made by wrapping maguey leaves around the lamb and sealing the pot with a paste of masa and water, I find that the more easily obtained corn husks trap plenty of steam in the pot above the meat and give the meat a subtle corn-scented aroma as well as eliminating the need to seal the pot with masa paste.

SERVES 4-6

1.25–1.5kg/2½–3lb lamb	½–1tsp dried oregano, crumbled
1 quantity Recado Rojo (page 18)	1l/1¾pt chicken stock
about 25 corn husks	**TO GARNISH**
1 medium onion, diced	3tbsp chopped fresh coriander
5 cloves garlic, chopped	1 small onion, chopped
400g/14oz tomatoes	1 lime, cut into wedges
30ml/2tbsp olive oil	
salt and pepper	

1. Coat the lamb in the Recado Rojo.
2. Soften the corn husks by pouring boiling water over them and leaving them, covered, for 30 minutes.
3. Place the lamb in a steamer with water or stock on the bottom. Cover the meat lightly with wet corn husks so that they fill the top part of the steamer pot.
4. Steam the meat over a very low heat until very tender, about 2 hours. Make sure that enough liquid remains at the bottom of the pot.
5. Meanwhile, purée the onion with the garlic and tomatoes in a blender or food processor.

6. Heat the oil in a saucepan and when nearly smoking add the onion-tomato purée. Cook until it changes colour and becomes less watery. Season with salt, pepper and oregano.
7. Add the stock and bring to the boil. Reduce the heat and simmer for 10 minutes.
8. Remove the corn husks from the meat, then remove the meat from the pan. Pour the juices from the bottom of the pan into the soup.
9. Cut the meat into small pieces and place in warm bowls. Ladle the soup over it and garnish with coriander, onion and wedges of lime.

NUTRITIONAL INFORMATION				
	TOTAL FAT	SAT FAT	CHOL	ENERGY
Total	168g	68g	1185mg	3085kcals/112928kJ
Per Serving (4)	42g	17g	296mg	771kcals/28232kJ
Per Serving (6)	28g	11.5g	198mg	514kcals/18821kJ

VARIATION

I like to serve birria with noodles, chickpeas or pinto beans, and courgettes to give substance and texture to the soup. Cook chopped courgettes in the simmering soup; thin noodles should be cooked separately and beans warmed in the soup with the meat and courgettes. To serve: place some noodles, courgettes and beans in each bowl then ladle hot soup and lamb over them. Garnish as suggested.

SOPA DE FRIJOLES CON CHIPOTLE Y LIMON

TARASCAN BEAN STEW
WITH CHIPOTLE AND LEMON

This spicy, lemony bean stew is one of my favourite vegetarian dishes, especially on a winter's night with a chunk of cheese oozing into delicious molten strings at the bottom of my bowl.

SERVES 4 – 6

½tsp cumin seeds	1l/1¾pt vegetable stock
1 onion, chopped	¼tsp oregano, crushed
15ml/1tbsp olive oil	**TO SERVE**
3–5 cloves garlic, chopped	chipotle en adobo marinade to taste
350g/12oz cooked drained beans, large white or pink such as pinto	1 lemon, cut into wedges
400g/14oz canned or fresh tomatoes, diced	

1. Toast the cumin seeds in an ungreased heavy-based frying pan until they are fragrant and lightly changed in colour. Take care they do not burn. Remove from the heat and crush. Set aside.
2. Lightly fry the onion in the olive oil until softened, then add the garlic and cook for a moment longer until fragrant but not browned.
3. Stir in the beans and tomatoes, cook in the fragrant oil for 1–2 minutes, then add the stock and simmer for 15–20 minutes. Remove about half the beans and mash or purée them, then return to the soup; season with oregano and toasted cumin seeds.
4. Serve the soup with a drizzle of chipotle marinade and a squeeze of lemon as desired.

NUTRITIONAL INFORMATION

	TOTAL FAT	SAT FAT	CHOL	ENERGY
Total	14g	2g	0mg	724kcals/3067kJ
Per Serving (4)	3.5g	0.5g	0mg	181kcals/767kJ
Per Serving (6)	2.3g	0.3g	0mg	121kcals/511kJ

POLLO TROPICALE

CARIBBEAN-STYLE CHICKEN AND VEGETABLE SOUP-STEW

A sprinkling of diced tomato and banana along with coconut and achiote give this unusual stew a decidedly tropical flavour. I've eaten similar soup-stews along the Caribbean coast, with seafood and fish instead of chicken.

SERVES 4 – 6

2 mild, fruity, smooth red chillies	75g/3oz creamed coconut, cut or scraped into small pieces
1 onion, unpeeled, halved	175–225g/6–8oz cooked chicken chunks or diced raw chicken breast
5 cloves garlic, unpeeled and whole	large pinch of dried oregano
2tsp achiote seeds ground to a powder or 1tbsp achiote paste, made by simmering and puréeing the seeds	pinch of ground cumin
	salt and pepper
7–8 canned or fresh ripe tomatoes	**TO SERVE**
15ml/1tbsp oil	½ ripe but firm banana
750ml/1¼pt chicken stock	juice from ½ a lime
1 courgette, cut into bite-sized pieces	1 lime, cut into wedges
175g/6oz sweetcorn kernels	1tbsp chopped fresh coriander
	1 medium tomato, diced

1. Place the chillies in a bowl and pour hot water over them. Leave to rest until they soften, about 30 minutes. When softened, remove the stems and seeds, then cut the flesh into small pieces. Purée in a blender or food processor, using just enough of the soaking liquid to make a purée.
2. Meanwhile, toast the onion and garlic under the grill until they are lightly charred.
3. When cool enough to handle, peel the onion and garlic, then dice and combine the achiote seeds and half the tomatoes. Purée in a blender or food processor.
4. Heat the oil in saucepan; when hot, pour in the puréed sauce and cook down until it is concentrated, paste-like, and darkened in colour. Do not let it burn.

5. Add the chicken stock and courgettes. Bring to the boil then reduce the heat and cook until the courgette is cooked through.

6. Add the sweetcorn, creamed coconut, chicken chunks, oregano and cumin and heat through. Stir every so often so that the creamed coconut melts. Add salt and pepper to taste.

7. Just before serving, dice the banana and toss with lime juice. Serve each bowlful of hot soup in a bowl with a sprinkling of banana, coriander, diced tomato, and wedges of lime. Offer hot pepper seasoning as desired.

NUTRITIONAL INFORMATION				
	TOTAL FAT	SAT FAT	CHOL	ENERGY
Total	83g	58g	75mg	1339kcals/5594kJ
Per Serving (4)	21g	14.5g	19mg	335kcals/1399kJ
Per Serving (6)	14g	9.5g	13mg	223kcals/9323kJ

CARNES, AVES Y PESCADOS

BRAISED, STEWED AND ROASTED DISHES

POLLO CON VERDOLOGAS EN CHILE ROJO

CHILLI AND PURSLANE CHICKEN

SERVES 4

1 chicken, cut into serving pieces	475ml/16fl oz boiling chicken stock
juice of 1 lime	45ml/3tbsp olive oil
2 cloves garlic, chopped	675g/1½lb tomatoes, toasted and lightly charred (page 8)
¼tsp dried oregano	2 heads of garlic, broken into cloves and peeled
¼tsp dried marjoram	
¼tsp dried thyme	1 bay leaf
¼tsp ground cumin	4tbsp masa harina or 2 tortillas
5 guajillo chillies, toasted and seeded, stems removed	handful of purslane or watercress
4 pasilla chillies, toasted and seeded, stems removed	

1. Rub the chicken with the lime juice, chopped garlic, oregano, marjoram, thyme, cumin and salt to taste. Leave for at least 1 hour.

2. Place the toasted chillies in a saucepan and pour the boiling stock over them. Cover and leave to rehydrate for 30 minutes or until they soften. Whirl the chillies, and just enough liquid as needed, in a blender or food processor until puréed.

3. Heat 15ml/1tbsp oil then pour in the chilli purée and cook until thickened and paste-like. Pour in the remaining soaking stock, simmer for a few minutes then set aside.

4. Brown the chicken pieces then arrange in a baking dish. Add any leftover juices from the marinade and the chilli sauce. Cover and simmer over low heat until the chicken is tender, about 25 minutes. (Breasts will cook quickly, dark meat will take longer. If desired, leave the breasts out for 10 minutes while dark meat cooks.)

5. Toast the masa harina in an ungreased heavy-based frying pan or toast the tortillas in the same manner and grind in a blender or food processor. Stir the toasted masa harina or ground tortillas into the sauce, adjusting the seasoning with a squirt of lime if needed and more stock if the sauce is too thick.

6. Just before serving, stir in the purslane or sprinkle with watercress.

NUTRITIONAL INFORMATION				
	TOTAL FAT	SAT FAT	CHOL	ENERGY
Total	81.6g	18.75g	630mg	1979kcals/8320kJ
Per Serving	20g	4.5g	158mg	495kcals/2080kJ

POLLO DEL JARDIN DE SAN MARCOS

SAN MARCOS CHICKEN

Aguascalientes, a small state in the centre of Mexico, is renowned for its fruit and vegetables, as well as the annual fête held in the Garden of San Marcos, in the capital city of the region.

SERVES 4

30ml/2tbsp olive oil

1 chicken, cut into serving pieces

1 onion, finely chopped

5 cloves garlic, chopped

675g/1½lb tomatoes, diced

475ml/16fl oz chicken stock

45–60ml/3–4tbsp vinegar

large pinch of sugar

large pinch of ground cloves

salt and pepper

¼tsp dried oregano or marjoram

2–3 large potatoes, par-boiled or steamed until half cooked then peeled and cut into slices or chunks

2 chorizos, skinned and broken into small pieces

1 cos lettuce

2 onions, finely chopped

1tsp capers

pickled jalapeño or serrano chillies (optional)

1. Heat the olive oil in a frying pan and lightly fry the chicken with 1 chopped onion and the garlic until the chicken is lightly golden and half-cooked. Remove from the heat.

2. In a blender or food processor, purée the tomatoes with the stock, vinegar, sugar, cloves, salt and pepper, oregano or marjoram. Place in a saucepan and bring to the boil. Reduce the heat and keep on a low simmer. Spoon about a third of the sauce over the chicken and return the chicken to the heat to finish cooking, covered, for another 15–25 minutes or so. If the chicken threatens to burn, add a little more oil or sauce.

3. Meanwhile, brown the potatoes with the chorizo.

4. Serve the cooked chicken on lettuce leaves, each portion with a spoonful or two of the potatoes and chorizo, chopped onion, capers, and pickled jalapeño or serrano chillies if using.

NUTRITIONAL INFORMATION			
	TOTAL FAT	SAT FAT	CHOL	ENERGY
Total	119.5g	37g	710mg	2451kcals/10272kJ
Per Serving	30g	9g	178mg	613kcals/2568kJ

POLLO CON RAJAS
CHILLI CHICKEN
WITH ROASTED GREEN PEPPER

SERVES 4

6 smooth-skinned mild red chillies	30ml/2tbsp vinegar
1½ onions, toasted in an ungreased heavy-based frying pan	⅛tsp dried thyme
	30ml/2tbsp olive oil
12–15 cloves garlic, toasted in an ungreased heavy-based frying pan	½tsp salt
	1 fresh or canned tomato, chopped
1tbsp ground achiote (page 19)	4 boneless, skinless chicken breasts, cut into strips
⅛–¼tsp ground cinnamon	3–4 onions, quartered
large pinch of ground cumin	2 green peppers, roasted, peeled and cut into strips
large pinch of black pepper	1 lime, cut into wedges
small pinch of ground cloves	fresh salsa of choice

1. Toast the chillies over an open flame until they catch fire. Let them burn for just a moment then blow out the flame. You want the chillies just slightly charred.

2. Remove the stems from the chillies and discard the seeds. Break the chillies into small pieces, place in a blender or food processor and purée with the toasted onions, garlic, achiote, cinnamon, cumin, black pepper, cloves, vinegar, thyme, half the olive oil, salt and tomato. Whirl until the mixture forms a paste.

3. Coat the chicken with the spice paste and leave to marinate for about 30 minutes.

4. In an ungreased heavy-based frying pan, lightly char the onion quarters, then remove from the pan. Add the remaining olive oil and fry the chicken strips, letting them cook quickly but not overcook. Remove from the pan. Quickly cook the peppers in the same pan then return the onions and chicken and warm through. Serve immediately, with lime and fresh salsa.

NUTRITIONAL INFORMATION

	TOTAL FAT	SAT FAT	CHOL	ENERGY
Total	37g	7.5g	172mg	892kcals/3739kJ
Per Serving	9g	2g	43mg	223kcals/935kJ

POLLO CON NOPALES Y CHILE ROJO

CHICKEN AND CACTUS
WITH RED CHILLI-GARLIC OIL

Marinating the chicken gives it flavour; poaching keeps it light, and the final tiny drizzle of chilli and garlic-infused oil gives it extra oomph.

This dish was inspired by the contemporary dishes coming out of Mexico these days: traditional ingredients and preparations with new thoughts and ideas, much in the same way the French kitchen went through changes in the 1970s and 1980s.

SERVES 4

1 chicken, cut into serving pieces, or 4–8 chicken breasts on the bone

1 quantity chilli-achiote seasoning paste from Pollo Rojo (page 50)

1 smooth-skinned flavourful dried chilli, crumbled

45ml/3tbsp olive oil

1 clove garlic, thinly sliced

750ml/1¼pt chicken stock

1 onion, halved and toasted

2–3 tomatoes, diced

225g/8oz cooked, drained cactus, cut into strips

1. Coat the chicken with seasoning paste. Make incisions all over the bird to ensure the seasonings really flavour the flesh. Leave to marinate overnight in the refrigerator.

2. To make the chilli oil, heat the chilli in a saucepan with the olive oil until small bubbles form at the edge of the pan. Remove from the heat and add the garlic. Leave to cool to room temperature, then strain. Set aside.

3. Bring the stock, onion and tomatoes to the boil in a large pan then reduce the heat. Add the chicken and simmer, covered, over a low heat, until tender, about 10 minutes for chicken breasts, 30 minutes for a whole chicken.

4. Serve the poached chicken in a bowl with the cactus and a little of the liquid puddled around it. Drizzle with a small amount of the red chilli-garlic oil and serve immediately.

NUTRITIONAL INFORMATION				
	TOTAL FAT	SAT FAT	CHOL	ENERGY
Total	80g	18.5g	630mg	1692 kcals/7097kJ
Per Serving	20g	4.5g	158mg	423kcals/1774kJ

POLLO Y ELOTE SUIZA

CHICKEN AND CORN
IN CREAMY CHILLI-TOMATO SAUCE

This creamy chicken dish is called Suiza (Swiss) because of the crème fraîche sauce – at one time anything that contained cream in Mexico was thought to have originated in Switzerland.

SERVES 4

1 chicken, cut into serving pieces

1tsp ground cumin

salt and pepper

15–30ml/1–2tbsp olive oil

5 cloves garlic, crushed or chopped

½–1 fresh red chilli such as jalapeño, thinly sliced

3 spring onions, thinly sliced

400g/14oz tomatoes, diced

250ml/8fl oz chicken stock

2 bay leaves

150–200g/5–7oz canned sweetcorn kernels, drained

350g/12oz crème fraîche or soured cream

1. Rub the chicken with cumin, salt and pepper and olive oil.

2. Heat an ungreased heavy-based frying pan and lightly brown the chicken, using the extra oil from rubbing it.

3. Add the garlic, red chilli and spring onions, then cover and cook over medium-low heat for about 10 minutes.

4. Add the tomatoes, cover, and continue to simmer until the chicken is cooked through, about 25 minutes.

5. Remove the chicken from the pan and place on a plate. Keep warm while you finish the sauce.

6. In a blender or food processor, purée the sauce with the chicken stock. Heat the remaining oil in a frying pan then pour in the puréed sauce, bay leaves and sweetcorn. Cook over high heat for about 5 minutes to reduce the sauce a little.

7. Stir in the crème fraîche or soured cream, then return the chicken to the pan along with any juices that have accumulated. Season with salt and pepper and warm through.

8. Serve hot, with a few spoonfuls of sauce.

NUTRITIONAL INFORMATION				
	TOTAL FAT	SAT FAT	CHOL	ENERGY
Total	133g	62g	855mg	2417kcals/10113kJ
Per Serving	33g	15.5g	214mg	604kcals/2528kJ

PICADILLO

SPICY-SWEET MEAT HASH
WITH ALMONDS AND GREEN OLIVES

Use picadillo to stuff into roasted green chillies for superb chillies rellenos, or roll a warm wheat tortilla around several spoonfuls of hot picadillo and a ladleful of black or red beans. Picadillo makes an excellent filling for empanadas, especially easily made empanadas using the very inauthentic but delicious filo dough for the pastry.

SERVES 6

900g/2lb lean minced beef	2–3 fresh green chillies, chopped
30ml/2tbsp vegetable oil, if needed	15–30ml/1–2tbsp vinegar
1–2 large onions, chopped	175ml/6fl oz sherry
5 cloves garlic, chopped	75–100g/3–4oz raisins
½tsp dried oregano	75–100g/3–4oz green pimento-stuffed olives, sliced or halved
½tsp ground cinnamon	
¼tsp ground cloves	75–100g/3–4oz toasted almonds, coarsely chopped or slivered
8 fresh or canned tomatoes, diced or chopped	
2–3tbsp sugar	3–4tbsp chopped fresh coriander

1. Fry the beef and onion until lightly browned. Add oil if needed, then stir in the onions, garlic, oregano, cinnamon, cloves and tomatoes and continue to cook for a few minutes longer.

2. Add the sugar, chillies, vinegar, sherry and raisins and cook over high heat until the liquid has evaporated by at least half.

3. Stir in the olives, almonds and coriander, taste for seasoning, and serve immediately.

NUTRITIONAL INFORMATION				
	TOTAL FAT	SAT FAT	CHOL	ENERGY
Total	137g	29g	590mg	2929kcals/12264kJ
Per Serving (6)	23g	5g	98mg	488kcals/2044kJ
Per Serving (8)	17g	3.5g	74mg	366kcals/1533kJ

POLLO CON SALSA DE CIRUELA

CHICKEN WITH PRUNES

Prunes make a rich, winey sauce, their sweetness balanced with the spicy, smoky chipotle chilli and the tangy edge of tamarind. Serve with boiled potatoes sprinkled with cumin and spring onions, or with steamed rice tossed with strips of roasted peeled green peppers and sautéed onions, with a sprinkling of cumin.

SERVES 4

1 chicken, cut into serving pieces	350ml/12fl oz chicken stock
juice of ½ lime or 4–6 crushed cooked tomatillos	10–12 prunes, stoned
	2–3tbsp sugar or honey
5 cloves garlic, chopped	1tbsp tamarind paste or Worcestershire sauce to taste
chipotle salsa or marinade from chipotle chillies, to taste	½tsp ground cinnamon
salt and pepper	¼tsp ground allspice or large pinch of ground cloves
flour for dusting	vinegar
vegetable oil	
6–8 tomatoes, diced	**TO GARNISH**
1 onion, chopped	2tbsp lightly toasted flaked almonds
120ml/4fl oz wine, beer or brandy	1tbsp chopped fresh coriander

1. Combine the chicken with the lime juice or tomatillos, half the garlic, the chipotle salsa and salt and pepper. Leave to marinate for 1 hour to overnight.

2. Dust the chicken with flour then lightly brown in oil in a frying pan, taking care it does not burn. Place in a casserole then pour out the fat from the frying pan.

3. Add the tomatoes, onion, wine, beer or brandy, chicken stock and remaining garlic to the frying pan and bring to the boil. Simmer for a few minutes until the onion turns translucent, then add the prunes, sugar or honey, tamarind paste or Worcestershire sauce, cinnamon, cloves, and chipotle to taste.

4. Pour the sauce into the casserole, letting it lightly coat the chicken and sink to the bottom of the casserole. Place the prunes under the chicken.

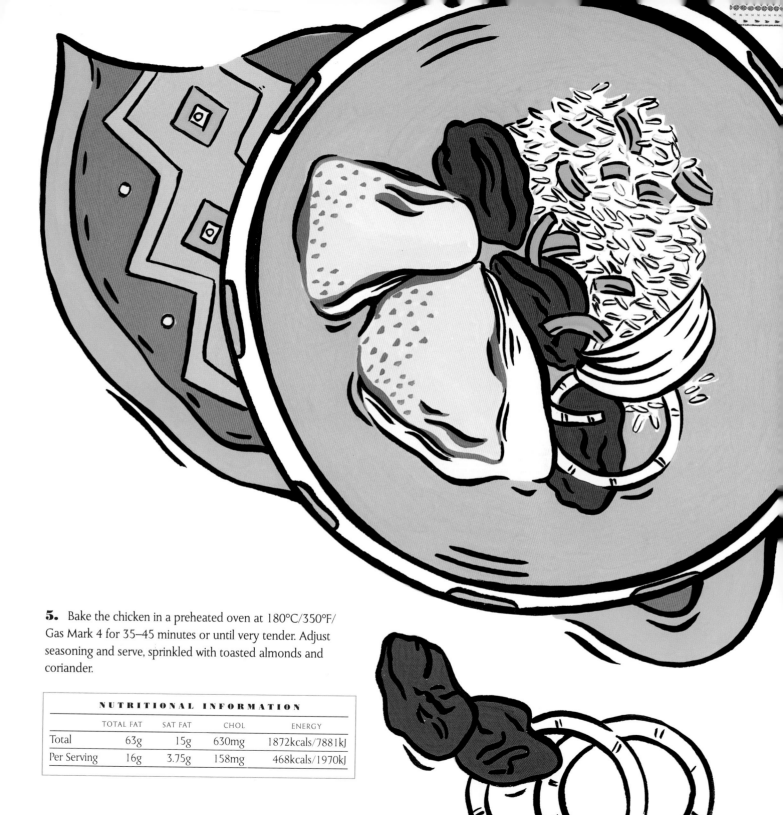

5. Bake the chicken in a preheated oven at 180°C/350°F/Gas Mark 4 for 35–45 minutes or until very tender. Adjust seasoning and serve, sprinkled with toasted almonds and coriander.

NUTRITIONAL INFORMATION				
	TOTAL FAT	SAT FAT	CHOL	ENERGY
Total	63g	15g	630mg	1872kcals/7881kJ
Per Serving	16g	3.75g	158mg	468kcals/1970kJ

MANCHAMANTEL

CHICKEN AND/OR PORK
IN MANCHAMANTEL SAUCE

Manchamantel is a type of bright red, fruit-redolent sauce, used for simmering chicken and/or pork. Its name translates as "tablecloth stainer" – perhaps because of its lurid colour, perhaps because in the enthusiasm of the moment, diners tend to spill a lot of the lovely sauce as they aim for their mouths. Manchamantel sauce can be prepared without the chicken or meat and used with foods grilled over coals: the richness of duck especially is nice with the fruity sauce.

SERVES 4

2 ancho chillies

1 guajillo chilli

475ml/16fl oz hot water

½ onion, toasted

3 cloves garlic, toasted

4 tomatoes, toasted and lightly charred

250ml/8fl oz meat or chicken stock, or ½–1 stock cube mixed with water

½tsp ground cinnamon

⅛tsp ground cloves

salt and pepper

15–30ml/1–2tbsp oil

15–30ml/1–2tbsp vinegar

1–2tsp sugar

450g/1lb boneless pork and ½ chicken, in serving pieces, or 900g/2lb pork, or 1 chicken

1 courgette or chayote, cut into bite-sized pieces

1 apple, preferably tart, peeled, cored and diced

½ carrot, thinly sliced

dried fruit: several tablespoons raisins, several prunes, a dried pear, apple and apricot (optional)

½ ripe pineapple, peeled and cut into bite-sized chunks

1 banana, diced

1. Toast the chillies on an open flame until they turn colour but do not blacken. Place in a pan of hot water and simmer for 20 minutes or until the chillies are softened.

2. Remove the stems and seeds and, in a blender or food processor, purée the chillies with enough of their soaking liquid to make a smooth purée.

3. Skin roast the onion and garlic (page 8) and dice; dice the tomatoes (leave on their charred skin – it adds flavour). Add the onion, garlic and tomatoes to the chilli purée and whirl to make a smooth sauce. Season with cinnamon, cloves and salt and pepper.

4. Heat the oil and when it is almost smoking pour in the sauce. Cook for a few minutes until it concentrates and darkens slightly, then add the vinegar, sugar, and pork if using both pork and chicken. If using only chicken, add that now.

5. Cook for about 45 minutes then add chicken and simmer a further 20–30 minutes.

6. Add the courgette or chayote, apple, carrot, dried fruit, if using, and pineapple. Continue to simmer until the fruit and meat are tender.

7. Adjust the seasoning and sugar-vinegar balance, then add the banana and warm through. Serve immediately.

NUTRITIONAL INFORMATION				
	TOTAL FAT	SAT FAT	CHOL	ENERGY
Total	72g	21g	660mg	2187kcals/9212kJ
Per Serving	18g	5g	165mg	547kcals/2303kJ

ALBONDIGAS CON CALABACITAS EN SALSA VERDE

MEATBALLS WITH COURGETTES AND POTATOES
IN GREEN TOMATILLO SAUCE

SERVES 4

450g/1lb lean minced beef

6tbsp cooked, drained rice or soft breadcrumbs

1 egg, lightly beaten

½ onion, finely chopped

3 cloves garlic, chopped

3–4tbsp chopped fresh coriander

4 guajillo chillies, toasted, seeded, stemmed and ground

½tsp ground cumin plus a pinch for the tomatillo sauce

salt and pepper

350g/12oz tomatillos, cooked and drained

1–2 fresh green chillies such as serrano

pinch of ground turmeric

15ml/1tbsp vinegar

30ml/2tbsp vegetable oil

475ml/16fl oz chicken or beef stock

1–2 large baking potatoes, peeled and cut into chunks

2–3 courgettes, sliced

TO SERVE

3tbsp fresh coriander

wedges of lemon or lime

1. Combine the meat with the rice or breadcrumbs, egg, onion, half the garlic, the chopped coriander, ground chilli powder, cumin and salt and pepper to taste. Roll into meatballs and set aside.

2. In a blender or food processor, purée the tomatillos with the remaining garlic, fresh chilli, pinch of cumin, turmeric and vinegar.

3. Heat the oil in a saucepan; when hot pour in the tomatillo mixture and cook until it reduces in volume and becomes a paste-like mixture.

4. Add the stock, potato and courgettes and carefully place the meatballs in the mixture. Cover and simmer over low heat for 20–30 minutes or until the vegetables are cooked through, occasionally basting the meatballs with the sauce. Taste for salt and pepper.

5. Serve in bowls, each sprinkled with coriander and accompanied by a wedge of lemon or lime.

NUTRITIONAL INFORMATION				
	TOTAL FAT	SAT FAT	CHOL	ENERGY
Total	55.5g	14.5g	533mg	1536kcals/6456kJ
Per Serving	14g	3.75g	133mg	384kcals/16144kJ

ALBONDIGAS EN SALSA ROJO CON LEGUMBRES

MEATBALLS IN SWEET-SPICY RED CHILLI SAUCE
WITH ASSORTED VEGETABLES

SERVES 4

225g/8oz each of minced pork and minced beef, or all minced beef

6tbsp cooked, drained rice or 3–4tbsp masa harina

1 egg, lightly beaten

1½ onion, finely chopped

3 cloves garlic, chopped

½tsp ground cumin

350ml/12fl oz stock

⅛–¼tsp ground cinnamon

2tbsp currants or raisins

½tbsp dark brown sugar

15–30ml/1–2tbsp vinegar

1 sweet potato, peeled and cut into chunks, or 5cm/2in slice of pumpkin, peeled and cut into chunks

1tsp chopped fresh parsley

1tbsp chopped fresh mint

large pinch of dried thyme

large pinch of ground cloves

salt and pepper

6 fresh or canned tomatoes

3tbsp ancho chilli powder

30ml/2tbsp vegetable oil

1 courgette or chayote, cut into chunks (if using chayote, peel and seed)

¼ cabbage, cut into chunks and blanched or par-boiled

1tbsp chipotle salsa or marinade from chipotles en adobo (optional)

2–3tbsp chopped fresh coriander

1. Mix the minced meat with the rice or breadcrumbs, egg, half the onion, half the garlic, and the parsley, cumin and mint and season with thyme, cloves and salt and pepper. Roll into egg-shaped meatballs and set aside.

2. In a blender or food processor, purée the tomatoes with the chilli powder and remaining onion and garlic. Heat the oil in a frying pan then pour in the puréed tomato-onion mixture and cook until it reduces and darkens slightly.

3. Add the stock, cinnamon, currants or raisins, brown sugar, vinegar, sweet potato or pumpkin, courgette or chayote and cabbage and mix well. Bring to the boil then reduce the heat to very low.

4. Gently place the meatballs in the mixture, cover, and simmer gently for 20–30 minutes, basting the meatballs occasionally with the sauce.

5. Adjust the seasoning of vinegar and brown sugar, check for salt, and add a little chilli powder or chipotle salsa or marinade to taste. Serve hot, in bowls, sprinkled with coriander, accompanied by either rice or tortillas.

NUTRITIONAL INFORMATION				
	TOTAL FAT	SAT FAT	CHOL	ENERGY
Total	62g	16g	558mg	1747kcals/7352kJ
Per Serving	15.5g	4g	139mg	437kcals/1838kJ

POLLO DE PLAZA ESTILO MORELIA

CHICKEN FROM THE PLAZA IN MORELIA

Surrounding the plaza in the colonial town of Morelia, vendors and restaurants offer pollo de plaza, a savoury concoction of chicken and enchiladas bathed in two sauces: red chilli and tomato.

SERVES 4

4 chicken breasts, on the bone	large pinch of ground allspice
½tsp dried thyme	large pinch of ground cumin
18 cloves garlic, chopped	vegetable oil
salt and pepper	675g/1½lb fresh or canned tomatoes, diced
2 bay leaves, crushed into a fine powder	12 tortillas
3–4 pasilla, ancho, or negro chillies	**TO SERVE**
1 onion, chopped	shredded cos lettuce
50ml/2fl oz vinegar	chopped onion
250ml/8fl oz boiling water	crumbled dried oregano
2 onions, chopped	crumbled Feta cheese
1tsp dried oregano	fresh serrano or jalapeño chilli, thinly sliced
large pinch of ground cinnamon	diced cooked carrots
	diced cooked potatoes

1. Coat the chicken with thyme, one-third of the garlic, salt and pepper, and bay leaves. Set aside.

2. To make the chilli sauce, toast the chillies in an ungreased heavy-based frying pan until they change colour slightly then remove the seeds and stems. Combine with the vinegar and water and leave to soften for 30 minutes.

3. Place the chillies in a blender or food processor with half the onion, one-third of the garlic, the oregano, cinnamon, allspice and cumin, and the soaking liquid. Whirl until the mixture forms a smooth sauce consistency.

4. Heat two tablespoons oil and pour in the chilli mixture. Cook over high heat until it reduces in volume and intensifies in flavour. Adjust the seasoning and set aside.

5. To make the tomato sauce, whirl the tomatoes, remaining onion and remaining garlic in a blender or food processor until smooth. Heat two tbsp oil in a frying pan and pour in the tomato mixture; season with sugar and salt and pepper to taste and cook until thickened and flavourful. Set aside.

6. Roast the chicken breasts in a casserole in a preheated oven at 160°C/325°F/Gas Mark 3 for about 15 minutes or pan brown in one–two tbsp oil.

7. To make the enchiladas, warm the tortillas in a small amount of oil then dip each one into the hot chilli sauce. Roll up immediately, arrange in a casserole and keep warm.

8. Serve the chicken sauced with a little tomato sauce, surrounded by enchiladas and chilli sauce, garnished with lettuce, onion, oregano, Feta cheese, fresh chilli, carrots and potatoes.

NUTRITIONAL INFORMATION				
	TOTAL FAT	SAT FAT	CHOL	ENERGY
Total	22g	5g	172mg	2297kcals/9745kJ
Per Serving	5.5g	1g	43mg	574kcals/2436kJ

PATO A LA NARANJA

DUCK ROASTED WITH ORANGES AND MILD RED CHILLI

SERVES 4

1 duck, prepared for roasting

salt and pepper

1 orange, washed and halved

1 lime, washed and halved

5–8 whole garlic cloves, unpeeled

60ml/4tbsp Recado Rojo (page 18) (or a paste of mild red chilli powder seasoned with garlic, cumin and chopped coriander, and thinned with a little orange juice)

1 onion, chopped

2 cloves garlic, chopped

3tbsp chopped fresh coriander

2 fresh green chillies such as serrano or jalapeño, chopped

juice of 2 oranges, plus about ½tsp of the grated zest

juice of ½ grapefruit, plus ⅛–¼tsp of the grated zest

juice of ½ lime

pinch of ground cumin

2tbsp sugar

120ml/4fl oz chicken, beef or duck stock

1. Place the duck in a roasting pan and sprinkle with salt and pepper all over. Lightly prick its skin evenly to help the fat drain off. Stuff with the orange and lime halves, whole garlic cloves, and 45ml/3tbsp Recado Rojo.

2. Roast in a preheated oven at 230°C/450°F/Gas Mark 8 for 20 minutes, then reduce the heat to 160°C/325°F/Gas Mark 3 and continue to cook for another hour so so or until the temperature reaches 180°C/350°F in its thigh. During the roasting, spoon or gently pour off the duck fat as it cooks (roast on a rack for allover crispness and easy draining). Save the duck fat for cooking potatoes and so on.

3. While the duck is cooking, make the salsa: combine the onion, garlic, coriander, chillies, half the orange juice and the zest, the grapefruit juice and zest and lime juice. Season with salt and cumin. Set aside.

4. Remove the duck from oven and place on a platter to allow it to settle for carving. Remove the stuffing ingredients and squeeze to extract their juices. Keep warm.

5. Spoon off any fat remaining in the pan. Add the juices from the platter and stuffing to the roasting pan, along with the remaining orange juice, the sugar and stock. Bring to the boil, stirring all the while to scrape up the crusty brown bits. Adjust the seasoning, adding more sugar or a dash of lime juice as needed.

6. Carve the duck and serve napped with the hot pan sauce and garnished with spoonfuls of the fresh salsa.

NUTRITIONAL INFORMATION				
	TOTAL FAT	SAT FAT	CHOL	ENERGY
Total	257g	70g	0mg	2856kcals/11808kJ
Per Serving	64g	17g	0mg	714kcals/2952kJ

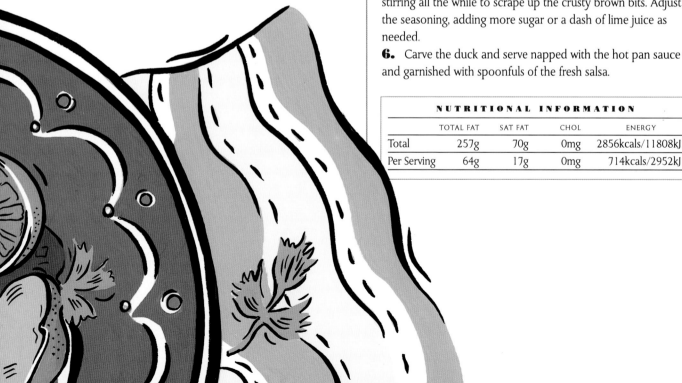

LOMO DE PUERCO

LOIN OF PORK BAKED IN SHARP-SOUR RED CHILLI SAUCE

Adobo, a red chilli sauce sharpened with vinegar and balanced with just a touch of sugar, is eaten with a variety of foods such as meats, fish and poultry. It is also often used as a pickling mixture, especially for chipotle, the feisty smoked chilli.

When meat and fish are prepared en adobo, they are usually first marinated in the mixture, then covered and baked until meltingly tender in the same mixture. This adobo permeates the flesh completely, an especially good technique where meat and poultry are old and tough, as they often are in rural regions of Mexico.

SERVES 4

4 large ancho chillies

475ml/16fl oz hot stock

1tsp ground cumin

several sprigs of fresh thyme

¼tsp dried oregano

5–8 cloves garlic, chopped

45ml/3tbsp orange juice

30ml/2tbsp red wine vinegar

½–1tsp chipotle marinade (optional)

pinch of ground allspice or cloves

1tbsp sugar

900g/2lb loin of pork

salt and pepper

TO SERVE

salsa of choice

chopped fresh coriander

soured cream

warm corn tortillas

1. Lightly toast the chillies over a hot flame until they change colour. Remove the stems and seeds and discard, and tear the chilli into small pieces, then combine with the hot stock to soften.

2. When the chillies have softened, whirl them in a blender or food processor with cumin, thyme, oregano, garlic, orange juice, vinegar, chipotle marinade, if using, a pinch of allspice or cloves, and sugar.

3. Sprinkle pork with salt and pepper then place in casserole and spoon sauce over it. Seal and roast in a preheated oven at 180°C/350°F/Gas Mark 4 for 2 hours then uncover and cook for another 30–45 minutes or until browned and crusty on top.

4. Serve with salsa of choice, chopped onions, coriander, soured cream and corn tortillas.

NUTRITIONAL INFORMATION				
	TOTAL FAT	SAT FAT	CHOL	ENERGY
Total	53g	19g	518mg	1197kcals/5015kJ
Per Serving	13g	4.5g	129mg	299kcals/1254kJ

CORDERO AL PASTOR

ROAST LAMB

WITH TEQUILA RED CHILLI SEASONING, GREEN OLIVES AND CRUMBLED CHEESE

The simple, strong flavours of this dish combine brilliantly. Serve with warm corn tortillas or crusty rolls (bolillos) and a salad of shredded lettuce, roasted mild green chillies and avocado.

SERVES 4

1–1½kg/2–3lb shoulder of lamb

1tsp paprika

1–2tbsp mild chilli powder

2tsp ground cumin

salt and pepper

6 cloves garlic, chopped

juice of 1 orange

juice of 1 lime or lemon

50ml/2fl oz tequila

475ml/16fl oz chicken or beef stock

1–2tsp sugar

TO GARNISH

175–225g/6–8oz crumbly cheese such as Queso Fresco, Pecorino, Lancashire or not-too-salty Feta

15 green olives, sliced

2tbsp coarsely chopped fresh coriander

1. Rub the lamb with the paprika, chilli powder, cumin, salt and pepper, half the garlic, the orange and lime or lemon juice and tequila. Leave to marinate for about an hour.

2. Place the lamb in a roasting tin and pour in half the stock. Place in a preheated oven at 180°C/350°F/Gas Mark 4. Cook the lamb until tender, basting from time to time, raising the heat at the end for about 10 minutes so that any fatty areas brown and crisp. Add more stock if the pan drippings threaten to burn or blacken.

3. Remove the lamb from the pan and leave to rest in a warm place while you make the sauce.

4. Spoon off all fat from the pan drippings, then add the remaining stock, the remaining garlic and the sugar. Bring to the boil. It should form a savoury sauce.

5. Slice the lamb and pour the sauce over it. Garnish with crumbled cheese, olives and coriander leaves. Serve immediately.

NUTRITIONAL INFORMATION				
	TOTAL FAT	SAT FAT	CHOL	ENERGY
Total	198g	139g	668mg	2694kcals/11203kJ
Per Serving	50g	35g	167mg	674kcals/2801kJ

LOMITOS

TENDER, SIMMERED, ORANGE-SAFFRON MARINATED PORK

This dish is from the Yucatan, where it is simmered in great cazuelas. In the marketplace in Merida you can buy it warm, served spooned on to fresh tortillas or thick masa cakes. Beef, lamb, or turkey thigh could be used in place of the pork.

SERVES 4 – 6

900g/2lb boneless pork, cut into pieces	salt and pepper
2tbsp mild chilli powder or mixture of sweet paprika and mild chilli	3 heads of garlic, unpeeled, cut into halves crosswise, toasted and lightly charred
3 cloves garlic, chopped	1 fresh green chilli, lightly charred
175ml/6fl oz orange juice	15ml/1tbsp oil
grated zest from ½ orange	1 onion, chopped
2 pinches of saffron	1 green pepper, chopped
juice of ½ lime	450g/1lb tomatoes, chopped
¼tsp cumin seeds	250ml/8fl oz water

1. Combine the pork with the chilli powder, garlic, orange juice, orange zest, saffron, lime juice, cumin seeds and salt and pepper. Leave to marinate in the refrigerator for 3 hours to overnight.

2. Peel the toasted garlic and coarsely chop. Remove the stems and seeds from the toasted chilli; peel and coarsely chop. Set aside.

3. Heat the oil in a frying pan and fry the onion, green pepper and tomatoes until the onion softens, then add the reserved garlic, green chilli, pork and water and simmer on low to medium heat until the meat is very tender and the sauce has evaporated to a thick paste-like sauce.

4. Adjust the seasoning and add a squeeze of orange/lime if needed. Serve immediately, with tortillas or rice and salad.

NUTRITIONAL INFORMATION				
	TOTAL FAT	SAT FAT	CHOL	ENERGY
Total	84.5g	27g	690mg	1810kcals/7581kJ
Per Serving (6)	21g	7g	173mg	452kcals/1895kJ
Per Serving (4)	17g	5g	138mg	362kcals/1516kJ

VARIATION
TACOS DE LOMITOS

Spoon on to homemade tortillas and top with a sprinkling of coriander and chopped slightly bitter salad greens such as endive.

ZANCAS DE CARDERO CON POSOLE

ROASTED LAMB SHANKS
POT-ROASTED WITH HOMINY

Rich chilli and tomato-spiced lamb, braised until moist and tender, is delicious with gentle hominy, all topped with the crisp freshness of shredded cabbage salad.

SERVES 4

4 lamb shanks or 1 shoulder roast

1 quantity red chilli paste, Recado Rojo (page 18)

1 onion, finely chopped

5 tomatoes, diced

1 red pepper, chopped

1 green pepper, chopped

250ml/8fl oz chicken or beef stock

100ml/4fl oz beer

1 lime, cut into wedges

½ cabbage, thinly sliced or shredded

olive oil and vinegar to taste

salt and pepper

350g/12oz cooked, drained hominy

¼tsp dried oregano

salsa of choice

1. Make incisions all over the lamb then coat with the red chilli paste. Leave to marinate for at least 1 hour, and preferably overnight.

2. Place in a baking dish and surround with the onion, tomatoes and red and green peppers. Pour in the stock and beer then cover the dish and bake in a preheated oven at 190°C/375°F/Gas Mark 4 for 2 hours or until the lamb is tender inside and crusty on the outside.

3. Meanwhile, dress the cabbage with oil and vinegar, salt and pepper, and set aside.

4. Pour off the fat from the baking dish, add the hominy to the pan juices and heat through. Serve the lamb and hominy with the pan juices, cabbage salad, and sprinkling of oregano. Accompany with a salsa of choice.

NUTRITIONAL INFORMATION				
	TOTAL FAT	SAT FAT	CHOL	ENERGY
Total	145g	105g	510mg	3032kcals/12656kJ
Per Serving	36g	26g	128mg	758kcals/3164kJ

COSTILLAS DE PUERCO
ROASTED SPARERIBS

The simplest meats are often the best. These spareribs should be juicy yet crispy, the fat having cooked right out of them, to be drained off.

SERVES 4

1.5–2.25kg/3–5lb spareribs, cut into separate pieces	salsa of choice such as Salsa de Pina (page 15)
salt and pepper	

1. Arrange the meat in a single layer in a baking dish and salt and pepper liberally. Add water to just cover.

2. Bake in a preheated oven at 150–160°C/300–325°F/Gas Mark 2–3 for about 3 hours, or until the water evaporates and the meat becomes crispy. Pour off excess fat every so often as the meat cooks. About 15 minutes before serving, toss with 4tbsp salsa, then return to the oven.

3. Adjust the seasoning and serve with salsa, tortillas, frijoles and guacamole.

VARIATION
SPARERIBS AND CLAMS WITH SALSA

Cook the meat as directed above; when it is almost done, add 3–5 clams per person. Toss the meat and clams with 3–5tbsp homemade mild salsa then raise the heat and return to the oven. Bake at 230°C/450°F/Gas Mark 8 for 15 minutes or until the clams open. Serve with extra salsa.

NUTRITIONAL INFORMATION				
	TOTAL FAT	SAT FAT	CHOL	ENERGY
Total	325g	164g	1080mg	4050kcals/16800kJ
Per Serving	81g	41g	270mg	1013kcals/4200kJ

CHICHARRON SUDADO EN SALSA VERDE

PORK BELLIES BRAISED IN GREEN SAUCE

This is a typical Tapatio or Guadaljaran dish, at its best when the meat is wrapped into soft tortillas for tacos.

SERVES 4

675g/1½lb pork belly, without rind, cut Into bite-sized pieces

1 quantity mild Salsa Verde de Tomatillo (page 15)

pinch of ground cumin

1 serrano chilli, thinly sliced

2tbsp chopped fresh coriander

1tbsp chopped onion

handful of purslane or watercress

1. Arrange the pork with the salsa in a baking dish. Cover and bake in a preheated oven at 160°C/325°F/Gas Mark 3 for 2–3 hours or until the meat is very tender. Spoon off the excess fat that rises to the surface.

2. Serve hot, sprinkled with cumin, chilli, coriander, onion and purslane or watercress. Accompany with tortillas.

NUTRITIONAL INFORMATION				
	TOTAL FAT	SAT FAT	CHOL	ENERGY
Total	152g	98g	540mg	2032kcals/8453kJ
Per Serving	38g	24.5g	135mg	508kcals/2113kJ

CALAMARES A LA VERACRUZANA

SQUID SIMMERED WITH TOMATOES, OLIVES AND CAPERS

Squid is very popular throughout the coastal regions of Mexico, either cooked on the barbecue or simmered with spicy tomato mixtures such as in this dish.

SERVES 4

900g/2lb cleaned squid, cut into rings and tentacles

30ml/2tbsp olive oil

salt

1 large onion, chopped

3 cloves garlic, chopped

900g/2lb ripe tomatoes, peeled and chopped (or use canned)

2 fresh green chillies, thinly sliced

1tbsp chopped fresh parsley

several sprigs of fresh thyme

several sprigs of fresh oregano or marjoram

1 bay leaf

⅛tsp ground cinnamon

pinch of ground allspice

pinch of sugar (optional)

1tbsp capers

15–20 green olives

1tbsp chopped fresh coriander

1. Lightly fry the squid in olive oil until it turns opaque. Season with salt and remove to a plate, leaving behind the flavoured oil in the pan.

2. Fry the onion and garlic in the squid-scented oil until softened, then stir in the tomatoes, chillies and herbs and season with cinnamon, allspice, and sugar if needed.

3. Cover and cook over medium-low heat until the mixture turns sauce-like and flavourful, about 5 minutes, then uncover the pan and cook for a further 5 minutes.

4. Stir in the reserved squid and any juices, along with the capers and olives. Warm through. Taste for seasoning, then serve immediately, sprinkled with coriander.

NUTRITIONAL INFORMATION				
	TOTAL FAT	SAT FAT	CHOL	ENERGY
Total	47g	9g	2250mg	1268kcals/5356kJ
Per Serving	12g	2g	563mg	317kcals/1389kJ

PESCADO DE LUJO DE MERIDA

FISH WITH TOMATO-CHIPOTLE CHILLI SAUCE

AND PLANTAINS MASHED WITH BACON

SERVES 4

4–6 steaks white firm-fleshed fish	⅛–¼tsp dried oregano
50ml/2fl oz lime juice	⅛–¼tsp ground cinnamon
¼tsp dried tarragon	extra chipotle chilli marinade (optional)
15–30ml/1–2tbsp olive oil	3–4 ripe but firm plantains, peeled and cut into bite-sized chunks
salt and pepper	
4 tomatoes, roasted in an ungreased pan	
Salsa de Muchos Chillies y Jitomate (page 18)	100g/4oz bacon or spicy smoked sausage, chopped

1. Arrange the fish steaks in a baking dish and sprinkle with lime juice, tarragon and salt and pepper.

2. Cover and bake for 15 minutes at190–200°C/375–400°F/ Gas Mark 5–6 or until it is just cooked through.

3. Meanwhile, purée the roasted tomatoes with the salsa in a blender or a food processor. Season with oregano and cinnamon, with extra chipotle if needed. Set the salsa aside.

4. Boil the plantains for 10 minutes or until just cooked through. At the same time, brown the bacon or sausage in its own fat until crispy. Mash the plantains and combine with the bacon or sausage and just enough of its own fat (or olive oil, or butter) to make a smooth, luscious mixture. Season with salt and pepper and cinnamon or oregano.

5. When the fish is cooked through, remove from the pan and splash it with the puréed tomato salsa. Serve with the mashed plantains.

NUTRITIONAL INFORMATION

	TOTAL FAT	SAT FAT	CHOL	ENERGY
Total	67.4g	22.5g	259mg	1935kcals/8166kJ
Per Serving	17g	5.5g	65mg	484kcals/2042kJ

PESCADO CON CILANTRO

FISH BAKED WITH LIME AND CORIANDER

SERVES 4

900g/2lb fillets of white fish such as snapper, bass, plaice or cod	1 large onion, chopped
	3 cloves garlic, chopped
salt and pepper	2–3 jalapeños en escabeche, chopped
85ml/3fl oz lime juice	25–50g/1–2oz fresh coriander, coarsely chopped
45ml/3tbsp olive oil	

1. Sprinkle the fish with salt and pepper then squeeze lime juice all over it.

2. Heat the olive oil in a frying pan and fry the onion and garlic until soft and lightly golden.

3. Arrange about a third of the onion mixture and a little of the chillies and coriander in a baking dish then place the fish on top. Top with the remaining onions, chillies and coriander.

4. Bake in a preheated oven at 180°C/350°F/Gas Mark 4 for about 15 minutes or until the fish has become slightly opaque and firmed. Serve immediately.

NUTRITIONAL INFORMATION

	TOTAL FAT	SAT FAT	CHOL	ENERGY
Total	40g	5.5g	460mg	1148kcals/4804kJ
Per Serving	10g	1g	115mg	287kcals/1201kJ

BRAISED, STEWED AND ROASTED DISHES

CAMARONES CON MANGUE
PRAWNS WITH MANGO

Here prawns are cooked in a brick-red mild chilli sauce, then served dotted with bits of sweet mango. Serve with a pile of warm, tender tortillas, and a pitcher of icy fruit and tequila drink.

SERVES 4

1 ancho chilli	juice of 1 lime
1 New Mexico or guajilla chilli	675g/1½lb prawns, shelled and cleaned
1 onion, halved but unpeeled	
3 cloves garlic, whole and unpeeled	**TO GARNISH**
4 fresh or canned tomatoes, diced	1 mango, peeled and diced
	1 fresh red chilli such as jalapeño, thinly sliced
pinch of ground cinnamon	1tbsp chopped fresh coriander
15–30ml/1–2tbsp oil	
250–350ml/8–12fl oz fish stock	½ lime, cut into wedges

1. Lightly toast the chillies in an ungreased heavy-based frying pan then pour over hot water to cover. Leave to rehydrate for at least 30 minutes. When softened, remove the stems and seeds, then slice the flesh and purée in a blender or food processor, using just enough soaking liquid to make a smooth paste.

2. Meanwhile, toast the onion and garlic in an ungreased heavy-based frying pan until lightly charred.

3. When the onion is cool enough to handle, peel and dice both onion and garlic, then purée with the tomatoes and cinnamon and add to the chilli purée.

4. Heat the oil in a frying pan, then pour in the purée and cook over medium high heat until it reduces, about 5–8 minutes.

5. Add the stock and simmer until it forms a smooth sauce. Add the lime juice and prawns. Cook for only 1–2 minutes until the prawns become pink and opaque. Do not overcook or they will be dry and unpleasant.

6. Serve the prawns and sauce garnished with mango, red chilli, coriander and wedges of lime.

NUTRITIONAL INFORMATION

	TOTAL FAT	SAT FAT	CHOL	ENERGY
Total	17g	2.5g	1463mg	844kcals/3558kJ
Per Serving	4g	0.5g	366mg	211kcals/890kJ

PIPIAN VERDE DE CAMARONES
PRAWNS IN GREEN PUMPKIN-SEED SAUCE

SERVES 4

175g/6oz pumpkin seeds, shelled but untoasted	½tsp ground cumin
	½tsp ground coriander
1 small or ½ medium onion, chopped	45ml/3tbsp olive oil
3 cloves garlic, chopped	250ml/8fl oz chicken stock
1–2tbsp chopped fresh coriander	675g/1½lb prawns, shelled
	30ml/2tbsp lime juice
350g/12oz tomatillos, cooked and drained	3 spring onions, thinly sliced, to garnish
1–2 chillies such as jalapeño, thinly sliced	

1. Grind the pumpkin seeds in a spice or coffee grinder then purée in a blender or food processor with the onion, garlic, fresh coriander, tomatillos, chillies, cumin and ground coriander.

2. Heat the oil in a frying pan then pour in this sauce and cook for about 5 minutes or until it reduces by about a third.

3. Pour in the stock and lower the heat, simmering until the sauce thickens slightly, then add the prawns and cook only until heated through and opaque pink rather than translucent.

4. Season to taste with lime juice, salt and pepper and serve sprinkled with spring onions.

NUTRITIONAL INFORMATION

	TOTAL FAT	SAT FAT	CHOL	ENERGY
Total	118g	18g	1463mg	1962kcals/8182kJ
Per Serving	30g	4g	366mg	491kcals/2045kJ

INDEX

Achiote Seasoning 19
Albondigas con Calabacitas en Salsa Verde 68–9
Albondigas en Salsa Rojo con Legumbres 69

Bacon-Wrapped Trout with Red Chilli Essence 51
Barbecued Chicken 50
Barbecued Clams with Salsa 57
Barbecued Duck Breasts with Mole 23
Barbecued Mussels in their Shells 57
Beef Stock & Meat 23
Birria 59

Calamares a la Veracruzano 76
Caldo de Pollo 21
Caldo de Puerco 21
Camarones con Mangue 79
Caldo del Res 23
Camarones Tropicales a la Parilla 54
Caribbean-Style Chicken & Vegetable Soup-Stew 60–1
Carne Asado con Platanos y Salsa 48
Carne Machaca 24–5
Carnitas 27
Chicharron Sudado en Salsa Verde 76
Chicken & Cactus with Red Chilli-Garlic Oil 64
Chicken Chilaquiles 33
Chicken & Corn in Creamy Chilli-Tomato Sauce 64
Chicken from the Plaza in Morelia 70
Chicken and/or Pork in Manchamantel Sauce 68
Chicken with Prunes 66–7
Chicken Stock 21
Chilaquiles con Pollo 33
Chilli Chicken with Roasted Green Pepper 63
Chilli & Purslane Chicken 61
Chilli-Tequila-Marinated Crisp Chicken Wings 53
Chipotle-Grilled Salmon with Three-Squash Salsa & Soured Cream 54
Chipotle-Onion Salsa Relish 15
Cocido 26
Cooked Tomato Sauce 17
Cordero al Pastor 72–3
Coriander & Lime Salsa 19
Corn Enchiladas 35
Corn Tortillas 10
Costillas de Puerco 75
Crispy Tender Pork 27

Dry Soup of Pasta in Mild Chilli Sauce with Cheese 39
Drunken Beans 13

Duck Roasted with Oranges & Mild Red Chilli 71

Eggs Scrambled with Tomatoes, Chillies & Tortillas 42
Enchiladas de Elotes 35
Enchiladas de Mole Rojo 38–9
Enchiladas in Red Mole 38–9
Enchiladas Verdes 35
  Pasilla-Painted 36

Fish Baked with Lime & Coriander 77
Fish Tamales with Watercress Salad 30
Fish with Tomato-Chipotle Chilli Sauce & Plantains Mashed with Bacon 77
Flour Tortillas 11
Frijoles Borachos 13
Frijoles de Olla 12–13
Frijoles Refritos 12
  con Queso 12

Goat's Cheese & Roasted Green Chilli Tamales 29
Green-Herbed Poussin with Roasted Red Pepper-Chipotle Cream 53
Green Salsa with Red Dried Chilli 19
Green-Tomato Enchiladas 36
  Pasilla-Painted 37
Grilled Rare Steak & Plantains 48

Hot Tomato Salsa with Vinegar 14
Huevos a la Mexicana 43
Huevos Motulenos 44
Huevos Oaxaquena 44
Huevos con Totopos (Migas) 42

Langosta a la Parilla 56
Layered Casserole of Shark & Tortillas, Campeche Style 34–5
Lobster Cooked on the Grill as in Rosarita Beach 56
Loin of Pork Baked in Sharp-Sour Red Chilli Sauce 72
Lomitos 73
  Tacos de 73
Lomo de Puerco 72

Manchamantel 68
Meatballs with Courgettes & Potatoes in Green Tomatillo Sauce 68–9
Meatballs in Sweet-Spicy Red Chilli Sauce 69
Mellejones 57
Mexican Eggs 43
Mild Red Chili Sauce 16
Mochomos 26–7
Mole 22–3
Mole Tacos 23

Oaxaca Eggs 44
Old Clothes in Tatters 24

Paella 40–1
Papadzules 34
Pan de Cazon 34–5
Patatas con Chipotle Crema y Queso de Cabrita 46
Pato a la Naranja 71
Pavo en Mole Poblano 22–3
Pescado Chipotle con Salsa de Calabacitas y Crema Acida 54
Pescado con Cilantro 77
Pescado de Lujo de Merida 77
Pescado a la Parilla 51
Picadillo 66
Pineapple Salsa 15
Pipian Verde de Camarones 79
Poc Chuc con Cebollas Asado 49
Pollito con Salsa Crema, Pimiento Rojo, y Chile Chipotle 53
Pollo con Chile y Tequila 53
Pollo y Elote Suiza 64
Pollo del Jardin de San Marcos 62
Pollo con Nopales y Chile Rojo 64
Pollo de Plaza Estilo Morelia 70
Pollo con Rajas 63
Polo Rojo a la Parilla 50
Pollo Rojo con Salsa de Aguacate 50
Pollo con Salsa de Ciruela 66–7
Pollo Tropicale 60–1
Pollo con Verdologas en Chile Rojo 61
Pork Bellies Braised in Green Sauce 76
Pork in Green Chilli Sauce 27
Posole 30–9
Posole de Hongos 31
Potatoes with Goat's Cheese-Chipotle Cream 46
Prawns in Green Pumpkin-Seed Sauce 79
Prawns with Mango 79
Puerco en Mole Verde 27

Recado Rojo 18
Red Chilli-Citrus Paste 18
Red Chilli-Marinated Chicken Breasts 50
Red Chilli-Seasoned Prawns with Tropical Fruit 54
Refried Beans 12
  with Cheese 12
Roast Lamb with Tequila Red Chilli Seasoning, Green Olives & Crumbled Cheese 72–3
Roasted Lamb Shanks, pot-roasted with Hominy 74
Roasted Spareribs 75
Ropa Vieja 24

Salsa de Chile Pasilla 16
Salsa Cruda 14
Salsa Cruda de Chipotle 15
Salsa Fria 14
Salsa de Limon y Cilantro 19
Salsa de Muchos Chiles y Jitomate 18
Salsa de Pina 15
Salsa Ranchera 17
Salsa of Roasted Tomatoes 18
Salsa Verde de Tomatillos 15 con Nopales 15
Salsa Verde de Tomatillo y Chilli Rojo 19
San Marcos Chicken 62
Shredded Beef with Seasoning 24–5
Shredded Pork with Guacamole 26–7
Simmered Beans 12–13
Simmered Dish of Meat, Vegetables & Fruit 26
Simmered Pork 21
Sopa de Frijoles con Chipotles y Limon 60
Sopa Seca de Fideos 39
Spicy-Sweet Meat Hash with Almonds & Green Olives 66
Squid Simmered with Tomatoes, Olives & Capers 76
Steamed Lamb served with a Savoury Broth 59

Tamales 28
Tamales de Pescado con Ensalada 30
Tamales de Queso de Cabrita 29
Tarascan Bean Stew with Chipotle & Lemon 60
Tender Simmered Orange-Saffron Marinated Pork 73
Tomatillo Salsa 15
  with Cactus 15
Tomato-Chilli Eggs 44
Tortillas de Harina 11
Tortillas de Maiz 10
Tostadas 11
Totopos (tortilla chips) 11
Turkey with Mole Sauce 22–3

Uncooked Salsa with Garlic & Tomato 14

Wild Mushroom Posole 31

Yucatecan Enchiladas of Hard-Boiled Egg & Pumpkin Seeds 34
Yucatan Steak 49

Zancas de Cardero con Posole 74

Index compiled by Sheila Seacroft